MW01028685

REVELATION
A Life Application® Bible Study

REVELATION
A LIFE APPLICATION® BIBLE STUDY

Part 1:
Complete text of Revelation with study notes from the
Life Application Study Bible
Part 2:
Thirteen lessons for individual or group study

Study questions written and edited by
Dr. Lyle Schrag
Rev. David R. Veerman
Dr. James C. Galvin
Dr. Bruce B. Barton

Tyndale House Publishers, Inc.
Wheaton, Illinois

Life Application Bible Studies

Matthew NIV	**1 Corinthians** NIV & NLT	**Hebrews** NIV
Mark NIV	**2 Corinthians** NIV	**James** NIV & NLT
Luke NIV	**Galatians & Ephesians** NIV & NLT	**1 & 2 Peter & Jude** NIV
John NIV & NLT	**Philippians & Colossians** NIV & NLT	**1 & 2 & 3 John** NIV
Acts NIV	**1 & 2 Thessalonians & Philemon** NIV	**Revelation** NIV & NLT
Romans NIV & NLT	**1 & 2 Timothy & Titus** NIV & NLT	

Visit Tyndale's exciting Web site at www.tyndale.com

Life Application Bible Studies: Revelation copyright © 1998 by Tyndale House Publishers, Inc., Wheaton, Illinois 60189. All rights reserved.

Life Application Notes and Bible Helps © 1986 owned by assignment by Tyndale House Publishers, Inc., Wheaton, Illinois 60189. Maps © 1986 by Tyndale House Publishers, Inc. All rights reserved.

Cover photo copyright © Pat O'Hara 1991. All rights reserved.

Life Application is a registered trademark of Tyndale House Publishers, Inc.

The text of Revelation is from the *Holy Bible*, New Living Translation, copyright © 1996 by Tyndale Charitable Trust. All rights reserved.

The text of the *Holy Bible,* New Living Translation, may be quoted in any form (written, visual, electronic, or audio) up to and inclusive of five hundred (500) verses without express written permission of the publisher, provided that the verses quoted do not account for more than 25 percent of the work in which they are quoted, and provided that a complete book of the Bible is not quoted.

When the *Holy Bible,* New Living Translation, is quoted, one of the following credit lines must appear on the copyright page or title page of the work:

Scripture quotations marked NLT are taken from the *Holy Bible,* New Living Translation, copyright © 1996. Used by permission of Tyndale House Publishers, Inc., Wheaton, Illinois 60189. All rights reserved.

Scripture quotations are taken from the *Holy Bible,* New Living Translation, copyright © 1996. Used by permission of Tyndale House Publishers, Inc., Wheaton, Illinois 60189. All rights reserved.

Unless otherwise indicated, all Scripture quotations are taken from the *Holy Bible,* New Living Translation, copyright © 1996. Used by permission of Tyndale House Publishers, Inc., Wheaton, Illinois 60189. All rights reserved.

When quotations from the NLT text are used in nonsalable media, such as church bulletins, orders of service, newsletters, transparencies, or similar media, a complete copyright notice is not required, but the initials NLT must appear at the end of each quotation.

Quotations in excess of five hundred (500) verses or 25 percent of the work, or other permission requests, must be approved in writing by Tyndale House Publishers, Inc. Send requests by e-mail to: permission@tyndale.com or call 630-668-8300, ext. 8817.

Publication of any commentary or other Bible reference work produced for commercial sale that uses the New Living Translation requires written permission for use of the NLT text.

TYNDALE, *New Living Translation, NLT,* and the New Living Translation logo are registered trademarks of Tyndale House Publishers, Inc.

ISBN 0-8423-3407-6

Printed in the United States of America

10 09 08 07 06 05
12 11 10   9   8   7

With 40 million copies in print, *The Living Bible* has been meeting a great need in people's hearts for more than thirty years. But even good things can be improved, so ninety evangelical scholars from various theological backgrounds and denominations were commissioned in 1989 to begin revising *The Living Bible*. The end result of this seven-year process is the *Holy Bible,* New Living Translation—a general-purpose translation that is accurate, easy to read, and excellent for study.

The goal of any Bible translation is to convey the meaning of the ancient Hebrew and Greek texts as accurately as possible to the modern reader. The New Living Translation is based on the most recent scholarship in the theory of translation. The challenge for the translators was to create a text that would make the same impact in the life of modern readers that the original text had for the original readers. In the New Living Translation, this is accomplished by translating entire thoughts (rather than just words) into natural, everyday English. The end result is a translation that is easy to read and understand and that accurately communicates the meaning of the original text.

We believe that this new translation, which combines the latest in scholarship with the best in translation style, will speak to your heart. We present the New Living Translation with the prayer that God will use it to speak his timeless truth to the church and to the world in a fresh, new way.

The Publishers
July 1996

Translation Philosophy and Methodology

There are two general theories or methods of Bible translation. The first has been called "formal equivalence." According to this theory, the translator attempts to render each word of the original language into the receptor language and seeks to preserve the original word order and sentence structure as much as possible. The second has been called "dynamic equivalence" or "functional equivalence." The goal of this translation theory is to produce in the receptor language the closest natural equivalent of the message expressed by the original-language text—both in meaning and in style. Such a translation attempts to have the same impact on modern readers as the original had on its own audience.

A dynamic-equivalence translation can also be called a thought-for-thought translation, as contrasted with a formal-equivalence or word-for-word translation. Of course, to translate the thought of the original language requires that the text be interpreted accurately and then be rendered in understandable idiom. So the goal of any thought-for-thought translation is to be both reliable and eminently readable. Thus, as a thought-for-thought translation, the New Living Translation seeks to be both exegetically accurate and idiomatically powerful.

In making a thought-for-thought translation, the translators must do their best to enter into the thought patterns of the ancient authors and to present the same ideas, connotations, and effects in the receptor language. In order to guard against personal biases and to ensure the accuracy of the message, a thought-for-thought translation should be created by a group of scholars who employ the best exegetical tools and who also understand the receptor language very well. With these concerns in mind, the Bible Translation Committee assigned each book of the Bible to three different scholars. Each scholar made a thorough review of the assigned book and submitted suggested revisions to the appropriate general reviewer. The general reviewer reviewed and summarized these suggestions and then proposed a first-draft revision of the text. This draft served as the basis for several additional phases of exegetical and stylistic committee review. Then the Bible Translation Committee jointly reviewed and approved every verse in the final translation.

A thought-for-thought translation prepared by a group of capable scholars has the potential to represent the intended meaning of the original text even more accurately than a word-for-word translation. This is illustrated by the various renderings of the Greek word *dikaiosune*. This term cannot be adequately translated by any single English word because it can connote human righteousness, God's righteousness, doing what is right, justice, being made right in God's sight, goodness, etc. The context—not the lexicon—must determine which English term is selected for translation.

The value of a thought-for-thought translation can be illustrated by comparing 2 Corinthians 9:1 in the King James Version, the New International Version, and the New Living Translation. "For as touching the ministering to the saints, it is superfluous for me to write to you" (KJV). "There is no need for me to write to you about this service to the saints" (NIV). "I really don't need to write to you about this gift for the Christians in Jerusalem" (NLT). Only the New Living Translation clearly translates the real meaning of the Greek idiom "service to the saints" into contemporary English.

Written to Be Read Aloud

It is evident in Scripture that the biblical documents were written to be read aloud, often in public worship (see Luke 4:16–20; 1 Timothy 4:13; Revelation 1:3). It is still the case today that more people will hear the Bible read aloud in church than are likely to read it for themselves. Therefore, a new translation must communicate with clarity and power when it is read aloud. For this reason, the New Living Translation is recommended as a Bible to be used for public reading. Its living language is not only easy to understand, but it also has an emotive quality that will make an impact on the listener.

The Texts behind the New Living Translation
The translators of the New Testament used the two standard editions of the Greek New Testament: the *Greek New Testament,* published by the United Bible Societies (fourth revised edition, 1993), and *Novum Testamentum Graece,* edited by Nestle and Aland (twenty-seventh edition, 1993). These two editions, which have the same text but differ in punctuation and textual notes, represent the best in modern textual scholarship.

Translation Issues
The translators have made a conscious effort to provide a text that can be easily understood by the average reader of modern English. To this end, we have used the vocabulary and language structures commonly used by the average person. The result is a translation of the Scriptures written generally at the reading level of a junior high school student. We have avoided using language that is likely to become quickly dated or that reflects a narrow subdialect of English, with the goal of making the New Living Translation as broadly useful as possible.

But our concern for readability goes beyond the concerns of vocabulary and sentence structure. We are also concerned about historical and cultural barriers to understanding the Bible, and we have sought to translate terms shrouded in history or culture in ways that can be immediately understood by the contemporary reader. Thus, our goal of easy readability expresses itself in a number of other ways:

- Rather than translating ancient weights and measures literally, which communicates little to the modern reader, we have expressed them by means of recognizable contemporary equivalents. We have converted ancient weights and measures to modern English (American) equivalents, and we have rendered the literal Greek measures, along with metric equivalents, in textual footnotes.

- Instead of translating ancient currency values literally, we have generally expressed them in terms of weights in precious metals. In some cases we have used other common terms to communicate the message effectively. For example, "three shekels of silver" might become "three silver coins" or "three pieces of silver" to convey the intended message. Again, a rendering of the literal Greek is given in textual footnotes.

- Since ancient references to the time of day differ from our modern methods of denoting time, we used renderings that are instantly understandable to the modern reader. Accordingly, we have rendered specific times of day by using approximate equivalents in terms of our common "o'clock" system. On occasion, translations such as "at dawn the next morning" or "as the sun began to set" have been used when the biblical reference is general.

- Many words in the original texts made sense to the original audience but communicate something quite different to the modern reader. In such cases, some liberty must be allowed in translation to communicate what was intended. Places identified by the term normally translated "city," for example, are often better identified as "towns" or "villages." Similarly, the term normally translated "mountain" is often better rendered "hill."

- Many words and phrases carry a great deal of cultural meaning that was obvious to the original readers but needs explanation in our own culture. For example, the phrase "they beat their breasts" (Luke 23:48) in ancient times meant that people were very upset. In our translation we chose to translate this phrase dynamically: "They went home *in deep sorrow.*" In some cases, however, we have simply illuminated the existing expression to make it immediately understandable. For example, we might have expanded the literal phrase to read "they beat their breasts *in sorrow.*"

- One challenge we faced was in determining how to translate accurately the ancient biblical text that was originally written in a context where male-oriented terms were used to refer to humanity generally. We needed to respect the nature of the ancient context while also trying to make the translation clear to a modern audience that tends to read male-oriented language as applying only to males. Often the original text, though using masculine nouns and pronouns, clearly intends that the message be applied to both men and women. One example is found in the New Testament epistles, where the believers are called "brothers" *(adelphoi).* Yet it is clear that these epistles were addressed to all the believers— male and female. Thus, we have usually translated this Greek word "brothers and sisters" in order to represent the historical situation more accurately.

  We have also been sensitive to passages where the text applies generally to human beings or to the human condition. In many instances we have used plural pronouns (they, them) in place of the masculine singular (he, him). For example, a traditional rendering of Proverbs 22:6 is: "Train up a child in the way he should go, and when he is old he will not turn from it." We have rendered it: "Teach your children to choose the right path, and when they are older, they will remain upon it." At times, we have also replaced third person pronouns with the second person to ensure clarity. A traditional rendering of Proverbs 26:27 is: "He who digs a pit will fall into it, and he who rolls a stone, it will come back on him." We have rendered it: "If you set a trap for others, you will get caught in it yourself. If you roll a boulder down on others, it will roll back on you." All such decisions were driven by the concern to reflect accurately the intended meaning of the original texts of Scripture.

  We should emphasize, however, that all masculine nouns and pronouns used to represent God (for example, "Father") have been maintained without exception. We believe that essential traits of God's revealed character can only be conveyed through the masculine language expressed in the original texts of Scripture.

Lexical Consistency in Terminology
For the sake of clarity, we have maintained lexical consistency in areas such as divine names, synoptic passages, rhetorical structures, and nontheological technical terms (i.e., liturgical, cultic, zoological, botanical, cultural, and legal terms). For theological terms, we have allowed a greater semantic range of acceptable English words or phrases for a single Greek word. We avoided weighty theological terms that do not readily communicate to many modern readers. For example, we avoided using words such as "justification," "sanctification," and "regeneration." In place of these words (which are carryovers from Latin), we provided renderings such as "we are made right with God," "we are made holy," and "we are born anew."

The Rendering of Divine Names
The Greek word *Christos* has been translated as "Messiah" when the context assumes a Jewish audience. When a Gentile audience can be assumed, *Christos* has been translated as "Christ." The Greek word *kurios* is consistently translated "Lord," except in four quotations of Psalm 110:1, where it is translated "LORD."

Textual Footnotes
The New Living Translation provides several kinds of textual footnotes:

- All Old Testament passages that are clearly quoted in the New Testament are identified in a textual footnote in the New Testament.

- Some textual footnotes provide cultural and historical information on places, things, and people in the Bible that are probably obscure to modern readers. Such notes should aid the reader in understanding the message of the text. For example, in Acts 12:1, "King Herod" is named in this translation as "King Herod

Agrippa" and is identified in a footnote as being "the nephew of Herod Antipas and a grandson of Herod the Great."

- When various ancient manuscripts contain different readings, these differences are often documented in footnotes. For instance, textual variants are footnoted when the variant reading is very familiar (usually through the King James Version). We have used footnotes when we have selected variant readings that differ from the Greek editions normally followed.

- Textual footnotes are also used to show alternative renderings. These are prefaced with the word "Or."

AS WE SUBMIT this translation of the Bible for publication, we recognize that any translation of the Scriptures is subject to limitations and imperfections. Anyone who has attempted to communicate the richness of God's Word into another language will realize it is impossible to make a perfect translation. Recognizing these limitations, we sought God's guidance and wisdom throughout this project. Now we pray that he will accept our efforts and use this translation for the benefit of the Church and of all people.

We pray that the New Living Translation will overcome some of the barriers of history, culture, and language that have kept people from reading and understanding God's Word. We hope that readers unfamiliar with the Bible will find the words clear and easy to understand, and that readers well versed in the Scriptures will gain a fresh perspective. We pray that readers will gain insight and wisdom for living, but most of all that they will meet the God of the Bible and be forever changed by knowing him.

The Bible Translation Committee
July 1996

WHY THE
LIFE APPLICATION STUDY BIBLE
IS UNIQUE

Have you ever opened your Bible and asked the following:

- What does this passage really mean?
- How does it apply to my life?
- Why does some of the Bible seem irrelevant?
- What do these ancient cultures have to do with today?
- I love God; why can't I understand what he is saying to me through his Word?
- What's going on in the lives of these Bible people?

Many Christians do not read the Bible regularly. Why? Because in the pressures of daily living they cannot find a connection between the timeless principles of Scripture and the ever-present problems of day-by-day living.

God urges us to apply his Word (Isaiah 42:23; 1 Corinthians 10:11; 2 Thessalonians 3:4), but too often we stop at accumulating Bible knowledge. This is why the *Life Application Study Bible* was developed—to show how to put into practice what we have learned.

Applying God's Word is a vital part of one's relationship with God; it is the evidence that we are obeying him. The difficulty in applying the Bible is not with the Bible itself, but with the reader's inability to bridge the gap between the past and present, the conceptual and practical. When we don't or can't do this, spiritual dryness, shallowness, and indifference are the results.

The words of Scripture itself cry out to us, "And remember, it is a message to obey, not just to listen to. If you don't obey, you are only fooling yourself" (James 1:22). The *Life Application Study Bible* helps us to obey God's Word. Developed by an interdenominational team of pastors, scholars, family counselors, and a national organization dedicated to promoting God's Word and spreading the gospel, the *Life Application Study Bible* took many years to complete. All the work was reviewed by several renowned theologians under the directorship of Dr. Kenneth Kantzer.

The *Life Application Study Bible* does what a good resource Bible should: It helps you understand the context of a passage, gives important background and historical information, explains difficult words and phrases, and helps you see the interrelationship of Scripture. But it does much more. The *Life Application Study Bible* goes deeper into God's Word, helping you discover the timeless truth being communicated, see the relevance for your life, and make a personal application. While some study Bibles attempt application, over 75 percent of this Bible is application-oriented. The notes answer the questions "So what?" and "What does this passage mean to me, my family, my friends, my job, my neighborhood, my church, my country?"

Imagine reading a familiar passage of Scripture and gaining fresh insight, as if it were the first time you had ever read it. How much richer your life would be if you left each Bible reading with a new perspective and a small change for the better. A small change every day adds up to a changed life—and that is the very purpose of Scripture.

The best way to define application is to first determine what it is *not.* Application is *not* just accumulating knowledge. Accumulating knowledge helps us discover and understand facts and concepts, but it stops there. History is filled with philosophers who knew what the Bible said but failed to apply it to their lives, keeping them from believing and changing. Many think that understanding is the end goal of Bible study, but it is really only the beginning.

Application is *not* just illustration. Illustration only tells us how someone else handled a similar situation. While we may empathize with that person, we still have little direction for our personal situation.

Application is *not* just making a passage "relevant." Making the Bible relevant only helps us to see that the same lessons that were true in Bible times are true today; it does not show us how to apply them to the problems and pressures of our individual lives.

What, then, is application? Application begins by knowing and understanding God's Word and its timeless truths. *But you cannot stop there.* If you do, God's Word may not change your life, and it may become dull, difficult, tedious, and tiring. A good application focuses the truth of God's Word, shows the reader what to do about what is being read, and motivates the reader to respond to what God is teaching. All three are essential to application.

Application is putting into practice what we already know (see Mark 4:24 and Hebrews 5:14) and answering the question "So what?" by confronting us with the right questions and motivating us to take action (see 1 John 2:5, 6 and James 2:26). Application is deeply personal—unique for each individual. It makes a relevant truth a personal truth and involves developing a strategy and action plan to live your life in harmony with the Bible. It is the biblical "how to" of life.

You may ask, "How can your application notes be relevant to my life?" Each application note has three parts: (1) an *explanation,* which ties the note directly to the Scripture passage and sets up the truth that is being taught; (2) the *bridge,* which explains the timeless truth and makes it relevant for today; (3) the *application,* which shows you how to take the timeless truth and apply it to your personal situation. No note, by itself, can apply Scripture directly to your life. It can only teach, direct, lead, guide, inspire, recommend, and urge. It can give you the resources and direction you need to apply the Bible, but only you can take these resources and put them into practice.

A good note, therefore, should not only give you knowledge and understanding but point you to application. Before you buy any kind of resource study Bible, you should evaluate the notes and ask the following questions: (1) Does the note contain enough information to help me understand the point of the Scripture passage? (2) Does the note assume I know more than I do? (3) Does the note avoid denominational bias? (4) Do the notes touch most of life's experiences? (5) Does the note help me apply God's Word?

NOTES

In addition to providing the reader with many application notes, the *Life Application Study Bible* offers several explanatory notes that help the reader understand culture, history, context, difficult-to-understand passages, background, places, theological concepts, and the relationship of various passages in Scripture to other passages.

BOOK INTRODUCTIONS

The Book Introduction is divided into several easy-to-find parts:

Timeline. A guide that puts the Bible book into its historical setting. It lists the key events and the dates when they occurred.

Vital Statistics. A list of straight facts about the book—those pieces of information you need to know at a glance.

Overview. A summary of the book with general lessons and applications that can be learned from the book as a whole.

Blueprint. The outline of the book. It is printed in easy-to-understand language and is designed for easy memorization. To the right of each main heading is a key lesson that is taught in that particular section.

Megathemes. A section that gives the main themes of the Bible book, explains their significance, and then tells why they are still important for us today.

Map. If included, this shows the key places found in that book and retells the story of the book from a geographical perspective.

OUTLINE

The *Life Application Study Bible* has a new, custom-made outline that was designed specifically from an application point of view. Several unique features should be noted:

1. To avoid confusion and to aid memory work, the book outline has only three levels for headings. Main outline heads are marked with a capital letter. Subheads are marked by a number. Minor explanatory heads have no letter or number.

2. Each main outline head marked by a letter also has a brief paragraph below it summarizing the Bible text and offering a general application.

3. Parallel passages are listed where they apply.

PROFILE NOTES

Among the unique features of this Bible are the profiles of key Bible people, including their strengths and weaknesses, greatest accomplishments and mistakes, and key lessons from their lives.

MAPS

The *Life Application Study Bible* has a thorough and comprehensive Bible atlas built right into the book. There are two kinds of maps: a book-introduction map, telling the story of the book, and thumbnail maps in the notes, plotting most geographic movements.

CHARTS AND DIAGRAMS

Many charts and diagrams are included to help the reader better visualize difficult concepts or relationships. Most charts not only present the needed information but show the significance of the information as well.

CROSS-REFERENCES

An updated, exhaustive cross-reference system in the margins of the Bible text helps the reader find related passages quickly.

TEXTUAL NOTES

Directly related to the text of the New Living Translation, the textual notes provide explanations on certain wording in the translation, alternate translations, and information about readings in the ancient manuscripts.

HIGHLIGHTED NOTES

In each Bible study lesson, you will be asked to read specific notes as part of your preparation. These notes have each been highlighted by a bullet (•) so that you can find them easily.

REVELATION

VITAL STATISTICS

PURPOSE:
To reveal the full identity of Christ and to give warning and hope to believers

AUTHOR:
The apostle John

TO WHOM WRITTEN:
The seven churches in Asia and all believers everywhere

DATE WRITTEN:
Approximately A.D. 95 from Patmos

SETTING:
Most scholars believe that the seven churches of Asia to whom John writes were experiencing the persecution that took place under Emperor Domitian (A.D. 90–95). It seems that the Roman authorities had exiled John to the island of Patmos (off the coast of Asia). John, who had been an eyewitness of the incarnate Christ, had a vision of the glorified Christ. God also revealed to him what would take place in the future—judgment and the ultimate triumph of God over evil.

KEY VERSE:
"God blesses the one who reads this prophecy to the church, and he blesses all who listen to it and obey what it says. For the time is near when these things will happen" (1:3).

KEY PEOPLE:
John, Jesus

KEY PLACES:
Patmos, the seven churches, the new Jerusalem

SPECIAL FEATURES:
Revelation is written in "apocalyptic" form—a type of Jewish literature that uses symbolic imagery to communicate hope (in the ultimate triumph of God) to those in the midst of persecution. The events are ordered according to literary, rather than strictly chronological, patterns.

WITH tiny wrinkles and cries, he entered the world and, wrapped in strips of cloth, took his first nap on a bed of straw. Subject to time and to parents, he grew to manhood in Roman-occupied Palestine, his gentle hands becoming strong and calloused in Joseph's woodworking shop. As a man, he walked through the countryside and city, touching individuals, preaching to crowds, and training 12 men to carry on his work. At every step he was hounded by those seeking to rid the world of his influence. Finally, falsely accused and tried, he was condemned to a disgraceful execution by foreign hands. And he died—spat upon, cursed, pierced by nails, and hung heavenward for all to deride. Jesus, the God-man, gave his life completely so that all might live.

At God's appointed time, the risen and ascended Lord Jesus will burst onto the world scene. Then everyone will know that Jesus is Lord of the universe! Those who love him will rejoice, greeting their Savior with hearts overflowing into songs of praise. But his enemies will be filled with fear. Allied with Satan, the enemies of Christ will marshal their legions against Christ and his armies. But who can withstand God's wrath? Christ will win the battle and reign victorious forever! Jesus, the humble suffering servant, is also the powerful, conquering King and Judge.

Revelation is a book of hope. John, the beloved apostle and eyewitness of Jesus, proclaimed that the victorious Lord would surely return to vindicate the righteous and judge the wicked. But Revelation is also a book of warning. Things were not as they should have been in the churches, so Christ called the members to commit themselves to live in righteousness.

Although Jesus gave this revelation of himself to John nearly 2,000 years ago, it still stands as a comfort and challenge to God's people today. We can take heart as we understand John's vision of hope: Christ will return to rescue his people and settle accounts with all who defy him.

John begins this book by explaining how he received this revelation from God (1:1–20). He then records specific messages from Jesus to the seven churches in Asia (2:1—3:22). Suddenly, the scene shifts as a mosaic of dramatic and majestic images bursts into view before John's eyes. This series of visions portrays the future rise of evil, culminating in the Antichrist (4:1—18:24). Then follows John's recounting of the triumph of the King of kings, the wedding of the Lamb, the final judgment, and the coming of the new Jerusalem (19:1—22:5). Revelation concludes with the promise of Christ's soon return (22:6–21), and John breathes a prayer that has been echoed by Christians through the centuries: "Amen! Come, Lord Jesus!" (22:20).

As you read the book of Revelation, marvel with John at the wondrous panorama of God's revealed plan. Listen as Christ warns the churches, and root out any sin that blocks your relationship with him. Be full of hope, knowing that God is in control, Christ's victory is assured, and all who trust him will be saved.

THE BLUEPRINT

A. LETTERS TO THE CHURCHES (1:1—3:22)

The vision John received opens with instructions for him to write to seven churches. He both commends them for their strengths and warns them about their flaws. Each letter was directed to a church then in existence but also speaks to conditions in the church throughout history. Both in the church and in our individual lives, we must constantly fight against the temptation to become loveless, immoral, lenient, compromising, lifeless, or casual about our faith. The letters make it clear how our Lord feels about these qualities.

B. MESSAGE FOR THE CHURCH (4:1—22:21)
  1. Worshiping God in heaven
  2. Opening the seven seals
  3. Sounding the seven trumpets
  4. Observing the great conflict
  5. Pouring out the seven plagues
  6. Seizing the final victory
  7. Making all things new

This revelation is both a warning to Christians who have grown apathetic and an encouragement to those who are faithfully enduring the struggles in this world. It reassures us that good will triumph over evil, gives us hope as we face difficult times, and gives guidance when we are wavering in our faith. Christ's message to the church is a message of hope for all believers in every generation.

MEGATHEMES

THEME	EXPLANATION	IMPORTANCE
God's Sovereignty	God is sovereign. He is greater than any power in the universe. God is not to be compared with any leader, government, or religion. He controls history for the purpose of uniting true believers in loving fellowship with him.	Though Satan's power may temporarily increase, we are not to be led astray. God is all-powerful. He is in control. He will bring his true family safely into eternal life. Because he cares for us, we can trust him with our very life.
Christ's Return	Christ came to earth as a "Lamb," the symbol of his perfect sacrifice for our sin. He will return as the triumphant "Lion," the rightful ruler and conqueror. He will defeat Satan, settle accounts with all those who reject him, and bring his faithful people into eternity.	Assurance of Christ's return gives suffering Christians the strength to endure. We can look forward to his return as king and judge. Since no one knows the time when he will appear, we must be ready at all times by keeping our faith strong.
God's Faithful People	John wrote to encourage the church to resist the demands to worship the Roman emperor. He warns all God's faithful people to be devoted only to Christ. Revelation identifies who the faithful people are and what they should be doing until Christ returns.	You can take your place in the ranks of God's faithful people by believing in Christ. Victory is sure for those who resist temptation and make loyalty to Christ their top priority.
Judgment	One day God's anger toward sin will be fully and completely unleashed. Satan will be defeated with all of his agents. False religion will be destroyed. God will reward the faithful with eternal life, but all who refuse to believe in him will face eternal punishment.	Evil and injustice will not prevail forever. God's final judgment will put an end to these. We need to be certain of our commitment to Jesus if we want to escape this great final judgment. No one who rejects Christ will escape God's punishment.
Hope	One day God will create a new heaven and a new earth. All believers will live with him forever in perfect peace and security. Those who have already died will be raised to life. These promises for the future bring us hope.	Our great hope is that what Christ promises will come true. When we have confidence in our final destination, we can follow Christ with unwavering dedication no matter what we must face. We can be encouraged by hoping in Christ's return.

A. LETTERS TO THE CHURCHES (1:1—3:22)

Near the end of his life, John received a vision from Christ, which he recorded for the benefit of the seven churches in Asia and for Christians throughout history. This is the only book in the Bible that promises a blessing to those who listen to its words and do what it says.

Prologue

1 This is a revelation from* Jesus Christ, which God gave him concerning the events that will happen soon. An angel was sent to God's servant John so that John could share the revelation with God's other servants. ²John faithfully reported the word of God and the testimony of Jesus Christ—everything he saw.

1:1 Or *of.*

1:1
Dan 2:28-29, 45
John 12:49; 17:8
Rev 1:19; 5:7;
17:1; 22:6, 8, 16

1:2
Rev 1:9; 6:9

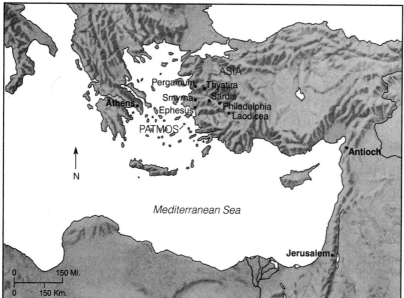

THE SEVEN CHURCHES
The seven churches were located on a major Roman road. A letter carrier would leave the island of Patmos (where John was exiled), arriving first at Ephesus. He would travel north to Smyrna and Pergamum, turn southeast to Thyatira, and continue on to Sardis, Philadelphia, and Laodicea—in the exact order in which the letters were dictated.

● **1:1** Revelation is a book about the future *and* about the present. It offers future hope to all believers, especially those who have suffered for their faith, by proclaiming Christ's final victory over evil and the reality of eternal life with him. It also gives present guidance as it teaches us about Jesus Christ and how we should live for him now. Through graphic pictures we learn that (1) Jesus Christ is coming again, (2) evil will be judged, and (3) the dead will be raised to judgment, resulting in eternal life or eternal destruction.

● **1:1** According to tradition, John, the author, was the only one of Jesus' original 12 disciples who was not killed for the faith. He also wrote the Gospel of John and the letters of 1, 2, and 3 John. When he wrote Revelation, John was in exile on the island of Patmos in the Aegean Sea, sent there by the Romans for his witness about Jesus Christ. For more information on John, see his Profile in John 13.

● **1:1** This book is the revelation *from, concerning,* and *of* Jesus Christ. God gave the revelation of his plan to Jesus Christ, who, in turn, revealed it to John. The book of Revelation unveils Christ's full identity and God's plan for the end of the world, and it focuses on Jesus Christ, his second coming, his victory over evil, and the establishment of his Kingdom. As you read and study Revelation, don't focus so much on the

timetable of the events or the details of John's imagery that you miss the main message—the infinite love, power, and justice of the Lord Jesus Christ.

● **1:1** The book of Revelation is *apocalyptic* (meaning uncovered, unveiled, or revealed) in style. This style of ancient literature usually featured spectacular and mysterious imagery, and such literature was written under the name of an ancient hero. John was acquainted with Jewish apocalyptic works, but his book is different in several ways: (1) He uses his own name rather than the name of an ancient hero; (2) he denounces evil and exhorts people to high Christian standards; (3) he offers hope rather than gloom. John was not a psychic attempting to predict the future; he was a prophet of God describing what God had shown him.

1:1 For more about angels, see the note on 5:11.

● **1:1** Jesus gave his message to John in a revelation (or vision), allowing John to see and record certain future events so they could be an encouragement to all believers. The vision includes many signs and symbols that convey the essence of what is to happen. What John saw, in most cases, was indescribable, so he used illustrations to show what it was *like.* When reading this symbolic language, we don't have to understand every detail—John himself didn't. Instead, realize that John's imagery shows us that Christ is indeed the glorious and victorious Lord of all.

1:3
Rev 22:7, 10

³God blesses the one who reads this prophecy to the church, and he blesses all who listen to it and obey what it says. For the time is near when these things will happen.

1:4
Exod 3:14
Rev 1:8; 3:1; 4:5,
8; 5:6; 11:17; 16:5

John's Greeting to the Seven Churches
⁴This letter is from John to the seven churches in the province of Asia. Grace and peace from the one who is, who always was, and who is still to come; from the sevenfold Spirit* before his throne; ⁵and from Jesus Christ, who is the faithful witness to these things, the first to rise from the dead, and the commander of all the rulers of the world.

1:5
Ps 89:27
Isa 40:2
Col 1:18
Rev 3:14; 19:11, 16

All praise to him who loves us and has freed us from our sins by shedding his blood

1:4 Greek *the seven spirits.*

INTERPRETING THE BOOK OF REVELATION	Approach	Description	Challenge	Caution
Over the centuries, four main approaches to interpreting the book of Revelation have developed. Each approach has had capable supporters, but none has proved itself the only way to read this book. However, the most basic application question for each approach can be summarized by asking yourself, Will this help me become a better follower of Jesus Christ today?	PRETERIST VIEW	John is writing to encourage Christians in his own day who are experiencing persecution from the Roman Empire.	To gain the same kind of encouragement John's first readers gained from the vivid images of God's sovereignty	Do not forget that most biblical prophecy has both an immediate and a future application.
	FUTURIST VIEW	Except for the first three chapters, John is describing events that will occur at the end of history.	To see in contemporary events many of the characteristics John describes and realize that the end could come at any time	Do not assume that we have "figured out" the future, since Jesus said that no one will know the day of his return before it happens.
	HISTORICIST VIEW	The book of Revelation is a presentation of history from John's day until the second coming of Christ and beyond.	To note the consistency of human evil throughout history and recognize that names may change but the rebellion against God has not	Be careful before identifying current events or leaders as fulfilling aspects of the book of Revelation.
	IDEALIST VIEW	The book of Revelation is a symbolic representation of the continual struggle of good and evil. It does not refer to any particular historical events. It is applicable at any point in history.	To gain insight into the past, to prepare for the future, and to live obediently and confidently in the present	Do not avoid the book because it is difficult. Try to understand Revelation within its broader literary context.

• **1:1-3** The book of Revelation reveals future events, but there is not the gloomy pessimism we might expect. The drama of these unfolding events is spectacular, but there is nothing to fear if you are on the winning side. When you think about the future, walk with confidence because Christ, the victor, walks with you.

• **1:3** Revelation is a book of prophecy that is both *prediction* (foretelling future events) and *proclamation* (preaching about who God is and what he will do). Prophecy is more than telling the future. Behind the predictions are important principles about God's character and promises. As we read, we will get to know God better so that we can trust him completely.

1:3 The typical news reports—filled with violence, scandal, and political haggling—are depressing, and we may wonder where the world is heading. God's plan for the future, however, provides inspiration and encouragement because we know he will intervene in history to conquer evil. John encourages churches to read this book aloud so everyone can hear it, apply it ("obey" it), and be assured of the fact that God will triumph.

• **1:3** When John says that "the time is near," he is urging his readers to be ready at all times for the last judgment and the establishment of God's Kingdom. We do not know when these events will occur, but we must always be prepared. They will happen quickly, and there will be no second chance to change sides.

• **1:4** Jesus told John to write to seven churches that knew and trusted him and had read his earlier letters (see 1:11). The letters were addressed so that they could be read and passed on in a

systematic fashion, following the main Roman road clockwise around the province of Asia (now called Turkey).

1:4 The "sevenfold Spirit" is another name for the Holy Spirit. The number seven is used throughout Revelation to symbolize completeness and perfection. For more about the Holy Spirit, see the notes on John 3:6 and Acts 1:5.

1:4-6 The Trinity—the Father ("the one who is, who always was, and who is still to come"), the Holy Spirit ("the sevenfold Spirit"), and the Son (Jesus Christ)—is the source of all truth (John 14:6, 17; 1 John 2:27; Revelation 19:11). Thus, we can be assured that John's message is reliable and is God's word to us.

1:5 Others had risen from the dead—people whom the prophets, Jesus, and the apostles had brought back to life during their ministries—but later those people died again. Jesus was the first who rose from the dead in an imperishable body (1 Corinthians 15:20), never to die again. He is the first to rise from the dead.

• **1:5, 6** Many hesitate to witness about their faith in Christ because they don't feel the change in their lives has been spectacular enough. But you qualify as a witness for Jesus because of what he has done for you, not because of what you have done for him. Christ demonstrated his great love by setting us free from our sins through his death on the cross ("freed us from our sins by shedding his blood for us"), guaranteeing us a place in his Kingdom, and making us priests to administer God's love to others. The fact that the all-powerful God has offered eternal life to you is nothing short of spectacular.

for us. ⁶He has made us his kingdom and his priests who serve before God his Father. Give to him everlasting glory! He rules forever and ever! Amen!

⁷Look! He comes with the clouds of heaven. And everyone will see him—even those who pierced him. And all the nations of the earth will weep because of him. Yes! Amen!

⁸"I am the Alpha and the Omega—the beginning and the end," says the Lord God. "I am the one who is, who always was, and who is still to come, the Almighty One."

Vision of the Son of Man

⁹I am John, your brother. In Jesus we are partners in suffering and in the Kingdom and in patient endurance. I was exiled to the island of Patmos for preaching the word of God and speaking about Jesus. ¹⁰It was the Lord's Day, and I was worshiping in the Spirit.* Suddenly, I heard a loud voice behind me, a voice that sounded like a trumpet blast. ¹¹It said, "Write down what you see, and send it to the seven churches: Ephesus, Smyrna, Pergamum, Thyatira, Sardis, Philadelphia, and Laodicea."

¹²When I turned to see who was speaking to me, I saw seven gold lampstands. ¹³And standing in the middle of the lampstands was the Son of Man.* He was wearing a long robe with a gold sash across his chest. ¹⁴His head and his hair were white like wool, as white as snow. And his eyes were bright like flames of fire. ¹⁵His feet were as bright as bronze refined in a furnace, and his voice thundered like mighty ocean waves. ¹⁶He held seven stars in his right hand, and a sharp two-edged sword came from his mouth. And his face was as bright as the sun in all its brilliance.

¹⁷When I saw him, I fell at his feet as dead. But he laid his right hand on me and said, "Don't be afraid! I am the First and the Last. ¹⁸I am the living one who died. Look, I

1:6
Isa 61:6
1 Pet 2:5, 9

1:7
Dan 7:13
Zech 12:10
Matt 24:30

1:8
Amos 3:13; 4:13

1:9
Phil 4:14
2 Tim 2:12

1:11
Rev 1:2, 19; 2:1, 18, 24; 3:1, 4, 7, 14

1:12
Zech 4:2

1:13
Ezek 9:2, 11
Dan 7:13; 10:5

1:14
Dan 7:9; 10:6

1:15
Ezek 1:24; 43:2

1:16
Isa 49:2

1:17
Isa 44:6; 48:12
Dan 8:18

1:10 Or *in spirit.*   **1:13** Or *one who looked like a man;* Greek reads *one like a son of man.* See Dan 7:13.

• **1:5-7** Jesus is portrayed as the all-powerful King, victorious in battle, glorious in peace. He is not just a humble earthly teacher, he is the glorious God. When you read John's description of the vision, keep in mind that his words are not just good advice; they are truth from the King of kings. Don't just read his words for their interesting and amazing portrayal of the future. Let the truth about Christ penetrate your life, deepen your faith in him, and strengthen your commitment to follow him no matter what the cost.

1:7 John is announcing the return of Jesus to earth (see also Matthew 24; Mark 13; 1 Thessalonians 4:15-18). Jesus' second coming will be visible and victorious. All people will see him arrive (Mark 13:26), and they will *know* it is Jesus. When he comes, he will conquer evil and judge all people according to their deeds (20:11-15).

1:7 "Those who pierced him" could refer to the Roman soldiers who pierced Jesus' side as he hung on the cross or to the Jews who were responsible for his death. John saw Jesus' death with his own eyes, and he never forgot the horror of it (see John 19:34, 35; see also Zechariah 12:10).

• **1:8** Alpha and omega are the first and last letters of the Greek alphabet. The Lord God is the beginning and the end. God the Father is the eternal Lord and Ruler of the past, present, and future (see also 4:8; Isaiah 44:6; 48:12-15). Without him you have nothing that is eternal, nothing that can change your life, nothing that can save you from sin. Is the Lord your reason for living, "the Alpha and the Omega" of your life? Honor the one who is the beginning and the end of all existence, wisdom, and power.

• **1:9** Patmos was a small rocky island in the Aegean Sea, about 50 miles offshore from the city of Ephesus on the Asia Minor seacoast (see map).

1:9 The Christian church was facing severe persecution. Almost all believers were socially, politically, or economically suffering because of this empire-wide persecution, and some were even being killed for their faith. John was exiled to Patmos because he refused to stop preaching the Good News. We may not face persecution for our faith as the early Christians did, but even with our freedom few of us have the courage to share God's Word with others. If we hesitate to share our faith during easy times, how will we do during times of persecution?

• **1:12, 13** The seven gold lampstands are the seven churches in Asia (1:11, 20), and Jesus stands among them. No matter what the churches face, Jesus protects them with his all-encompassing love and reassuring power. Through his Spirit, Jesus Christ is still among the churches today. When a church faces persecution, it should remember Christ's deep love and compassion. When a church is troubled by internal strife and conflict, it should remember Christ's concern for purity and his intolerance of sin.

1:13, 14 This "Son of Man" is Jesus himself. The title *Son of Man* occurs many times in the New Testament in reference to Jesus as the Messiah. John recognized Jesus because he lived with him for three years and had seen him both as the Galilean preacher and as the glorified Son of God at the Transfiguration (Matthew 17:1-8). Here Jesus appears as the mighty Son of Man. His white hair indicates his wisdom and divine nature (see also Daniel 7:9); his bright eyes symbolize judgment of all evil; the gold sash across his chest reveals him as the High Priest, who goes into God's presence to obtain forgiveness of sin for those who have believed in him.

1:16 The sword in Jesus' mouth symbolizes the power and force of his message. His words of judgment are as sharp as swords (Isaiah 49:2; Hebrews 4:12).

• **1:17, 18** As the Roman government stepped up its persecution of Christians, John must have wondered if the church could survive and stand against the opposition. But Jesus appeared in glory and splendor, reassuring John that he and his fellow believers had access to God's strength to face these trials. If you are facing difficult problems, remember that the power available to John and the early church is also available to you (see 1 John 4:4).

• **1:17, 18** Our sins have convicted and sentenced us, but Jesus holds the keys of death and the grave. He alone can free us from eternal bondage to Satan. He alone has the power and authority to set us free from sin's control. Believers don't have to fear death or the grave because Christ holds the keys to both. All we must do is turn from sin and turn to him in faith. When we attempt to control our life and disregard God, we set a course that leads directly to hell. But when we place our life in Christ's hands, he restores us now and resurrects us later to an eternal, peaceful relationship with him.

1:19
Isa 48:6
Rev 1:1

1:20
Rev 1:4, 12, 16;
2:1; 3:1

am alive forever and ever! And I hold the keys of death and the grave.* ¹⁹ Write down what you have seen—both the things that are now happening and the things that will happen later. ²⁰This is the meaning of the seven stars you saw in my right hand and the seven gold lampstands: The seven stars are the angels of* the seven churches, and the seven lampstands are the seven churches.

The Message to the Church in Ephesus

2:1
Rev 1:12-16, 20;
3:1

2 " Write this letter to the angel of* the church in Ephesus. This is the message from the one who holds the seven stars in his right hand, the one who walks among the seven gold lampstands:

1:18 Greek *and Hades.*   **1:20** Or *the messengers for.*   **2:1** Or *the messenger for;* also in 2:8, 12, 18.

A JOURNEY THROUGH THE BOOK OF REVELATION
Revelation is a complex book, and it has baffled interpreters for centuries. We can avoid a great deal of confusion by understanding the literary structure of this book. This approach will allow us to understand the individual scenes within the overall structure of Revelation and keep us from getting unnecessarily bogged down in the details of each vision. John gives hints throughout the book to indicate a change of scene, a change of subject, or a flashback to an earlier scene.

In chapter 1, John relates the circumstances that led to the writing of this book (1:1–20). In chapters 2 and 3, Jesus gives special messages to the seven churches of Asia Minor (2:1—3:22).

Suddenly, John is caught up into heaven, where he sees a vision of God Almighty on his throne. All of Christ's followers and the heavenly angels are worshiping God (4:1–11). John watches as God gives a scroll with seven seals to the worthy Lamb, Jesus Christ (5:1–14). The Lamb begins to open the seals one by one. As each seal is opened, a new vision appears.

As the first four seals are opened, riders appear on horses of different colors: war, famine, disease, and death are in their path (6:1–8). As the fifth seal is opened, John sees those in heaven who have been martyred for their faith in Christ (6:9–11).

A set of contrasting images appears at the opening of the sixth seal. On one side, there is a great earthquake, stars fall from the sky, and the sky rolls up like a scroll (6:12–17). On the other side, multitudes are before the throne, worshiping and praising God and the Lamb (7:1–17).

Finally, the seventh seal is opened (8:1–5), unveiling a series of God's judgments announced by seven angels with seven trumpets. The first four angels bring hail, fire, a mountain of fire, and a falling star—the sun and moon are darkened (8:6–13). The fifth trumpet announces the coming of locusts with the power to sting (9:1–12). The sixth trumpet heralds the coming of an army of warriors on horses (9:13–21). In 10:1–11, John is given a small scroll to eat. Following this, John is commanded to measure the Temple of God (11:1, 2). He sees two witnesses, who proclaim God's judgment on the earth for three and a half years (11:3–14).

Finally, the seventh trumpet sounds, calling the rival forces of good and evil to the final battle. On one side is Satan and his forces; on the other side stands Jesus Christ with his forces (11:15—13:18). In the midst of this call to battle, John sees three angels announcing the final judgment (14:6–13). Two angels begin to reap this harvest of judgment on the earth (14:14–20). Following on the heels of these two angels are seven more angels, who pour out God's judgment on the earth from seven bowls (15:1—16:21). One of these angels from the group of seven reveals to John a vision of a "great prostitute" called Babylon (symbolizing the Roman Empire), riding a scarlet beast (17:1–18). After the defeat of Babylon (18:1–24), a great multitude in heaven shouts praise to God for his mighty victory (19:1–10).

The final three chapters of the book of Revelation catalog the events that finalize Christ's victory over the enemy: Satan's 1,000-year imprisonment (20:1–10), the final judgment (20:11–15), and the creation of a new earth and a new Jerusalem (21:1—22:6). An angel then gives John final instructions concerning the visions John has seen and what to do once he has written them all down (22:7–11).

Revelation concludes with the promise of Christ's soon return, an offer to drink of the water of life that flows through the great street of the new Jerusalem, and a warning to those who read the book (22:12–21). May we pray with John, "Amen! Come, Lord Jesus!" (22:20).

The Bible ends with a message of warning and hope for men and women of every generation. Christ is victorious, and all evil has been done away with. As you read the book of Revelation, marvel at God's grace in the salvation of the saints and his power over the evil forces of Satan, and remember the hope of this victory to come.

1:20 Who are the "angels of the seven churches"? Some say that they are angels designated to guard the churches; others say that they are elders or pastors of the local churches. Because the seven letters in chapters 2 and 3 contain reprimands, it is doubtful that these angels are heavenly messengers. If these are earthly leaders or messengers, they are accountable to God for the churches they represent.

2:1 Ephesus was the capital of Asia Minor, a center of land and sea trade, and, along with Alexandria and Antioch in Syria,

one of the three most influential cities in the eastern part of the Roman Empire. The temple to Artemis, one of the ancient wonders of the world, was located in this city, and a major industry was the manufacture of images of this goddess (see Acts 19:21-41). Paul ministered in Ephesus for three years and warned the Ephesians that false teachers would come and try to draw people away from the faith (see Acts 20:29-31). False teachers did indeed cause problems in the Ephesian church, but the church resisted them, as we can see from Paul's letter

2 " I know all the things you do. I have seen your hard work and your patient endurance. I know you don't tolerate evil people. You have examined the claims of those who say they are apostles but are not. You have discovered they are liars. ³You have patiently suffered for me without quitting. ⁴But I have this complaint against you. You don't love me or each other as you did at first! ⁵Look how far you have fallen from your first love! Turn back to me again and work as you did at first. If you don't, I will come and remove your lampstand from its place among the churches. ⁶But there is this about you that is good: You hate the deeds of the immoral Nicolaitans, just as I do.

⁷"Anyone who is willing to hear should listen to the Spirit and understand what the Spirit is saying to the churches. Everyone who is victorious will eat from the tree of life in the paradise of God.

2:2
2 Cor 11:13
1 Jn 4:1
Rev 2:19

2:3
John 15:21

2:4
Jer 2:2
Matt 24:12

2:5
Rev 2:16, 22; 3:3, 19

2:6
Ps 139:21

2:7
Gen 2:8-9; 3:22-24
Ezek 31:8-9

---

to the Ephesians. John spent much of his ministry in this city and knew that they had resisted false teaching (2:2).

2:1 The one who "walks among the seven gold lampstands" (the seven churches) is Jesus (1:11-13). He holds the "seven stars in his right hand" (messengers of the churches), indicating his power and authority over the churches and their leaders. Ephesus had become a large, proud church, and Jesus' message would remind them that he alone is the head of the body of believers.

● **2:1ff** Does God care about your church? If you are tempted to doubt it, look more closely at these seven letters. The Lord of the universe knew each of these churches and its precise situation. In each letter, Jesus told John to write about specific people, places, and events. He praised believers for their successes and told them how to correct their failures. Just as Jesus cared for each of these churches, he cares for yours. He wants it to reach its greatest potential. The group of believers with whom you worship and serve is God's vehicle for changing the world. Take it seriously—God does.

● **2:2** Over a long period of time, the church in Ephesus had steadfastly refused to tolerate sin among its members. This was not easy in a city noted for immoral sexual practices associated with the worship of the goddess Artemis. We also are living in times of widespread sin and sexual immorality. It is popular to be open-minded toward many types of sin, calling them personal choices or alternative life-styles. But when the body of believers begins to tolerate sin in the church, it is lowering the standards and compromising the church's witness. Remember that God's approval is infinitely more important than the world's.

● **2:2, 3** Christ commended the church at Ephesus for (1) working hard, (2) patiently enduring, (3) not tolerating evil people, (4) critically examining the claims of false apostles, and (5) suffering without quitting. Every church should have these characteristics. But these good efforts should spring from our love for Jesus Christ. Both Jesus and John stressed love for one another as an authentic proof of the Good News (John 13:34; 1 John 3:18, 19). In the battle to maintain sound teaching and moral and doctrinal purity, it is possible to lose a charitable spirit. Prolonged conflict can weaken or destroy our patience and affection. In defending the faith, guard against any structure or rigidity that weakens love.

● **2:4** Paul had once commended the church at Ephesus for its love for God and others (Ephesians 1:15), but many of the church founders had died, and many of the second-generation

believers had lost their zeal for God. They were a busy church—the members did much to benefit themselves and the community—but they were acting out of the wrong motives. Work for God must be motivated by love for God, or it will not last.

● **2:4, 5** Just as when a man and woman fall in love, so also new believers rejoice at their newfound forgiveness. But when we lose sight of the seriousness of sin, we begin to lose the thrill of our forgiveness (see 2 Peter 1:9). In the first steps of your Christian life, you may have had enthusiasm without knowledge. Do you now have knowledge without enthusiasm? Both are necessary if we are to keep love for God intense and untarnished (see Hebrews 10:32, 35). Do you love God with the same fervor as when you were a new Christian?

● **2:5** For Jesus to "remove your lampstand from its place" would mean the church would cease to be an effective church. Just as the seven-branched candlestick in the Temple gave light for the priests to see, the churches were to give light to their surrounding communities. But Jesus warned them that their lights could go out. In fact, Jesus himself would extinguish any light that did not fulfill its purpose. The church needed to repent of its sins.

● **2:6** The Nicolaitans were believers who compromised their faith in order to enjoy some of the sinful practices of Ephesian society. The name *Nicolaitans* is held by some to be roughly the Greek equivalent of the Hebrew word for "Balaamites." Balaam was a prophet who induced the Israelites to carry out their lustful desires (see 2:14 and Numbers 31:16). When we want to take part in an activity that we know is wrong, we may make excuses to justify our behavior, saying that it isn't as bad as it seems or that it won't hurt our faith. Christ has strong words for those who look for excuses to sin.

● **2:6** Through John, Jesus commended the church at Ephesus for hating the wicked practices of the Nicolaitans. Note that they didn't hate the people, just their sinful actions. We should accept and love all people and refuse to tolerate any evil. God cannot tolerate sin, and he expects us to stand against it. The world needs Christians who will stand for God's truth and point people toward right living.

2:7 We are victorious by believing in Christ, persevering, remaining faithful, and living as one who follows Christ. Such a life brings great rewards (21:7).

2:7 Two trees were in the Garden of Eden—the tree of life and the tree of the knowledge of good and evil (see Genesis 2:9). Eating from the tree of life brought eternal life with God; eating from the tree of knowledge brought realization of good and evil. When Adam and Eve ate from the tree of knowledge, they disobeyed God's command. So they were excluded from Eden and barred from eating from the tree of life. Eventually, evil will be destroyed and believers will be brought into a restored paradise. In the new earth, everyone will eat from the tree of life and live forever.

The Message to the Church in Smyrna

2:8
Rev 1:11, 17-18

[8] " Write this letter to the angel of the church in Smyrna. This is the message from the one who is the First and the Last, who died and is alive:

2:9
2 Cor 6:10;
11:14-15
Rev 3:9

[9] " I know about your suffering and your poverty—but you are rich! I know the slander of those opposing you. They say they are Jews, but they really aren't because theirs is a synagogue of Satan. [10] Don't be afraid of what you are about to

2:10
Dan 1:12, 14
Jas 1:12
Rev 3:9; 17:14

suffer. The Devil will throw some of you into prison and put you to the test. You will be persecuted for 'ten days.' Remain faithful even when facing death, and I will give you the crown of life.

2:11
Rev 2:7; 20:6, 14

[11] "Anyone who is willing to hear should listen to the Spirit and understand what the Spirit is saying to the churches. Whoever is victorious will not be hurt by the second death.

The Message to the Church in Pergamum

2:12
Rev 1:16; 2:16

[12] " Write this letter to the angel of the church in Pergamum. This is the message from the one who has a sharp two-edged sword:

THE NAMES OF JESUS

Reference	Jesus' Name	Reference	Jesus' Name
1:13	The Son of Man	7:17	Shepherd
1:17	The First and the Last	12:10	Christ
1:18	The living one who died	19:11	Faithful and True
2:18	The Son of God	19:13	The Word of God
3:14	The faithful and true witness	19:16	King of kings
4:11	Creator	19:16	Lord of lords
5:5	The Lion of the tribe of Judah	22:13	The Alpha and the Omega
5:5	The root of David	22:13	The Beginning and the End
5:6	Lamb	22:16	The bright morning star

Scattered among the vivid images of the book of Revelation is a large collection of names for Jesus. Each one tells something of his character and highlights a particular aspect of his role within God's plan of redemption.

2:8 The city of Smyrna was about 25 miles north of Ephesus. It was nicknamed "Port of Asia" because it had an excellent harbor on the Aegean Sea. The church in this city struggled against two hostile forces: a Jewish population strongly opposed to Christianity, and a non-Jewish population that was loyal to Rome and supported emperor worship. Persecution and suffering were inevitable in an environment like this.

2:9, 10 Persecution comes from Satan, not from God. Satan, the Devil, will cause believers to be thrown into prison and even killed. But believers need not fear death, because it will only result in their receiving the crown of life. Satan may harm their earthly bodies, but he can do them no spiritual harm. The "synagogue of Satan" means that these Jews were serving Satan's purposes, not God's, when they gathered to worship. "Ten days" means that although persecution would be intense, it would be relatively short. It would have a definite beginning and end, and God would remain in complete control.

2:9-11 Pain is part of life, but it is never easy to suffer, no matter what the cause. Jesus commended the church at Smyrna for its faith in suffering. He then encouraged the believers that they need not fear the future if they remained faithful. If you are experiencing difficult times, don't let them turn you away from God. Instead, let them draw you toward greater faithfulness. Trust God and remember your heavenly reward (see also 22:12-14).

2:10 Smyrna was famous for its athletic games. A crown was the victory wreath, the trophy for the champion at the games. If we have been faithful, we will receive the prize of victory—eternal life (James 1:12). The message to the Smyrna church was to remain faithful during suffering because God is in control and his promises are reliable. Jesus never says that by being faithful to him we will avoid troubles, suffering, and persecution. Rather, we must be faithful to him *in* our sufferings. Only then will our faith prove to be genuine. We remain faithful by keeping our eyes on Christ and on what he promises us now and in the future (see Philippians 3:13, 14; 2 Timothy 4:8).

2:11 Believers and unbelievers alike experience physical death. All people will be resurrected, but believers will be resurrected to eternal life with God while unbelievers will be resurrected to be punished with a second death, eternal separation from God (see also 20:14; 21:8, 27; 22:15).

2:12 The city of Pergamum was built on a hill 1,000 feet above the surrounding countryside, creating a natural fortress. It was a sophisticated city, a center of Greek culture and education, with a 200,000-volume library. But it was also the center of four cults, and it rivaled Ephesus in its worship of idols. The city's chief god was Asclepius, whose symbol was a serpent and who was considered the god of healing. People came to Pergamum from all over the world to seek healing from this god.

2:12 Just as the Romans used their swords for authority and judgment, Jesus' sharp two-edged sword represents God's ultimate authority and judgment. It may also represent God's future separation of believers from unbelievers. Unbelievers cannot experience the eternal rewards of living in God's Kingdom.

13" I know that you live in the city where that great throne of Satan is located, and yet you have remained loyal to me. And you refused to deny me even when Antipas, my faithful witness, was martyred among you by Satan's followers. 14And yet I have a few complaints against you. You tolerate some among you who are like Balaam, who showed Balak how to trip up the people of Israel. He taught them to worship idols by eating food offered to idols and by committing sexual sin. 15In the same way, you have some Nicolaitans among you—people who follow the same teaching and commit the same sins. 16Repent, or I will come to you suddenly and fight against them with the sword of my mouth.

17"Anyone who is willing to hear should listen to the Spirit and understand what the Spirit is saying to the churches. Everyone who is victorious will eat of the manna that has been hidden away in heaven. And I will give to each one a white stone, and on the stone will be engraved a new name that no one knows except the one who receives it.

The Message to the Church in Thyatira

18" Write this letter to the angel of the church in Thyatira. This is the message from the Son of God, whose eyes are bright like flames of fire, whose feet are like polished bronze:

19" I know all the things you do—your love, your faith, your service, and your patient endurance. And I can see your constant improvement in all these things. 20But I have this complaint against you. You are permitting that woman—that Jezebel who calls herself a prophet—to lead my servants astray. She is encouraging them to worship

2:13
Rev 14:12

2:14
Num 31:16
1 Cor 6:13
2 Pet 2:15
Jude 1:11

2:15
Rev 2:6

2:16
2 Thes 2:8
Rev 1:16; 2:5;
22:7, 12, 20

2:17
Ps 78:24
Isa 62:2; 65:15
John 6:49-58
Rev 3:12; 19:12

2:18
Dan 10:6
Rev 1:14-15

2:19
Rev 2:2

2:20
1 Kgs 16:31
2 Kgs 9:7, 22

• **2:13** As the center for four idolatrous cults (Zeus, Dionysius, Asclepius, and Athene), Pergamum was called the city "where that great throne of Satan is located." Surrounded by worship of Satan and the Roman emperor as god, the church at Pergamum refused to renounce its faith, even when Satan's worshipers martyred one of its members. Standing firm against the strong pressures and temptations of society is never easy, but the alternative is deadly (2:11).

2:13-15 It was not easy to be a Christian in Pergamum. Believers experienced great pressure to compromise or leave the faith. (For information on the Nicolaitans, see the first note on 2:6.) Nothing is known about Antipas except that he did *not* compromise. He was faithful, and he died for his faith. Apparently, however, some in the church were tolerating those who taught or practiced what Christ opposed. Compromise can be defined as a blending of the qualities of two different things or a concession of principles. Cooperate with people as much as you can, but avoid any alliance, partnership, or participation that could lead to immoral practices.

• **2:14** There is room for differences of opinion among Christians in some areas, but there is no room for heresy and moral impurity. Your town might not participate in idol feasts, but it probably has pornography, sexual sin, cheating, gossiping, and lying. Don't tolerate sin by bowing to the pressure to be open-minded.

2:14-16 Balak was a king who feared the large number of Israelites traveling through his country, so he hired Balaam to pronounce a curse on them. Balaam refused at first, but an offer of money changed his mind (Numbers 22–24). Later Balaam influenced the Israelites to turn to idol worship (Numbers 31:16; also see 2 Peter 2:15; Jude 1:11). Here Christ rebuked the church for tolerating those who, like Balaam, lead people away from God.

2:16 This sword is God's judgment against rebellious nations (19:15, 21) and all forms of sin. See also the note on 1:16 and the second note on 2:12.

2:17 This "manna that has been hidden away in heaven" suggests the spiritual nourishment that the faithful believers will receive. As the Israelites traveled toward the Promised Land, God provided manna from heaven for their physical nourishment (Exodus 16:13-18). Jesus, as the bread of life (John 6:51), provides spiritual nourishment that satisfies our deepest hunger.

2:17 It is unclear what the white stones are or exactly what the name on each will be. Because they relate to the hidden manna, they may be symbols of the believer's eternal nourishment or

eternal life. The stones are significant because each will bear the new name of every person who truly believes in Christ. They are the evidence that a person has been accepted by God and declared worthy to receive eternal life. A person's name represented his or her character. God will give us a new name and a new heart.

2:18 Thyatira was a working person's town, with many trade guilds for cloth making, dyeing, and pottery. Lydia, Paul's first convert in Philippi, was a merchant from Thyatira (Acts 16:14). The city was basically secular, with no focus on any particular religion.

2:19 The believers in Thyatira were commended for growing in good deeds. We should not only take comfort in gathering for worship or rejoice when people give their lives to Christ in our church. We should also seek to grow in love, faith, and acts of service. Because the times are critical, we must spend our days wisely and faithfully.

2:20 A woman in the church in Thyatira was teaching that immorality was not a serious matter for believers. Her name may have been Jezebel, or John may have used the name Jezebel to symbolize the kind of evil she was promoting. Jezebel, a pagan queen of Israel, was considered the most evil woman who ever lived (see 1 Kings 19:1, 2; 21:1-15; 2 Kings 9:7-10, 30-37; and her Profile in 1 Kings 21).

• **2:20** Why is sexual immorality serious? Sex outside marriage always hurts someone. It hurts God because it shows that we prefer to satisfy our desires our own way instead of according to God's Word or to satisfy them immediately instead of waiting for his timing. It hurts others because it violates the commitment so necessary to a relationship. It hurts us because it often brings disease to our bodies and adversely affects our personalities. Sexual immorality has tremendous power to destroy families, churches, and communities because it destroys the integrity on which these relationships are built. God wants to protect us from hurting ourselves and others; thus, we are to have no part in sexual immorality, even if our culture accepts it.

2:20 In pagan temples, meat was often offered to idols. Then the meat that wasn't burned was sold to shoppers in the temple marketplace. Eating meat offered to idols wasn't wrong in itself, but it could violate the conscience of weaker Christian brothers and sisters who would be bothered by it (see 1 Corinthians 8 and the note on Romans 14:2). Jezebel was obviously more concerned about her own selfish pleasure and freedom than about the needs and concerns of fellow believers.

2:21
Rev 9:20

2:22
Rev 17:2; 22:9

2:23
Prov 24:12
Jer 17:10
Matt 16:27
Luke 16:15
Rom 8:27

2:25
Rev 3:11

2:26-27
Ps 2:8-9
Matt 10:22
Rev 12:5

2:28
Rev 22:16

2:29
Rev 2:7

3:1
Rev 1:4, 11, 16;
3:8, 15

3:3
Matt 24:42-44
Luke 22:32
1 Thes 5:2-6
2 Pet 3:10
Rev 2:5; 16:15

idols, eat food offered to idols, and commit sexual sin. 21 I gave her time to repent, but she would not turn away from her immorality. 22 Therefore, I will throw her upon a sickbed, and she will suffer greatly with all who commit adultery with her, unless they turn away from all their evil deeds. 23 I will strike her children dead. And all the churches will know that I am the one who searches out the thoughts and intentions of every person. And I will give to each of you whatever you deserve. 24 But I also have a message for the rest of you in Thyatira who have not followed this false teaching ('deeper truths,' as they call them—depths of Satan, really). I will ask nothing more of you 25 except that you hold tightly to what you have until I come.

26 " To all who are victorious, who obey me to the very end, I will give authority over all the nations. 27 They will rule the nations with an iron rod and smash them like clay pots. 28 They will have the same authority I received from my Father, and I will also give them the morning star! 29 Anyone who is willing to hear should listen to the Spirit and understand what the Spirit is saying to the churches.

The Message to the Church in Sardis

3 " Write this letter to the angel of* the church in Sardis. This is the message from the one who has the sevenfold Spirit* of God and the seven stars:

" I know all the things you do, and that you have a reputation for being alive—but you are dead. 2 Now wake up! Strengthen what little remains, for even what is left is at the point of death. Your deeds are far from right in the sight of God. 3 Go back

3:1a Or *the messenger for;* also in 3:7, 14.   **3:1b** Greek *the seven spirits.*

THE LETTERS TO THE SEVEN CHURCHES	Church	Reference	Commendation	Rebuke	Action
	Ephesus	2:1–7	Hard work, perseverance	Forsaken first love	Remember and repent
	Smyrna	2:8–11	Suffered persecution, poverty	None	Don't fear; be faithful
	Pergamum	2:12–17	True to faith	Compromise	Repent
	Thyatira	2:18–29	Love, faith, service	Immorality	Repent
	Sardis	3:1–6	Effective	Superficial	Wake up; repent
	Philadelphia	3:7–13	Faithful	None	Hold on
	Laodicea	3:14–22	None	Lukewarm	Be earnest and repent

This summary of the letters to the seven churches shows us the qualities our churches should seek and those we should avoid.

2:21 Jezebel was unwilling to repent. *Repent* means "to change one's mind and to turn from sin" and its disastrous consequences to God and eternal life. In his mercy, God has given us time to decide to follow him. Only our stubborn willfulness stands in the way.

2:23 We cannot hide from Christ; he knows what is in our heart and mind, and still he loves us. The sins we try to hide from God need to be confessed to him.

2:24, 25 The "deeper truths" of Satan were either false teaching advocated by heretics, or secret insights by so-called believers "guaranteed" to promote deeper spiritual life. We should hold tightly to the basics of our Christian faith and view with caution and counsel any new teaching that turns us away from the Bible, the fellowship of our church, or our basic confession of faith.

2:26, 27 Christ says that those who overcome (those who remain faithful until the end and continue to please God) will rule over Christ's enemies and reign with him as he judges evil (see also Psalm 2:8, 9; Isaiah 30:14; Jeremiah 19:11; 1 Corinthians 6:2, 3; Revelation 12:5; 19:15; 20:3, 4 for more about God's judgment).

2:28 Christ is also called the morning star in 22:16. A morning star appears just before dawn, when the night is coldest and darkest. When the world is at its bleakest point, Christ will burst onto the scene, exposing evil with his light of truth and bringing his promised reward.

3:1 The wealthy city of Sardis was actually in two locations. The older section of the city was on a mountain, and when its population outgrew the spot, a newer section was built in the valley below.

3:1 The "sevenfold Spirit" is another name for the Holy Spirit. The seven stars are the messengers, or leaders, of the churches (see the note on 2:1).

3:1 The problem in the Sardis church was not heresy but spiritual death. In spite of its reputation for being active, Sardis was infested with sin. Its deeds were evil, and its clothes soiled. The Spirit has no words of commendation for this church that looked so good on the outside but was so corrupt on the inside.

• **3:3** The church at Sardis was urged to obey the Christian truth they had heard when they first believed in Christ, to get back to the basics of the faith. It is important to grow in our knowledge of the Lord, to deepen our understanding through careful study. But no matter how much we learn, we must never abandon the basic truths about Jesus. Jesus will always be God's Son, and his sacrifice for our sins is permanent. No new truth from God will ever contradict these fundamental biblical teachings.

to what you heard and believed at first; hold to it firmly and turn to me again. Unless you do, I will come upon you suddenly, as unexpected as a thief.

4 " Yet even in Sardis there are some who have not soiled their garments with evil deeds. They will walk with me in white, for they are worthy. 5 All who are victorious will be clothed in white. I will never erase their names from the Book of Life, but I will announce before my Father and his angels that they are mine. 6 Anyone who is willing to hear should listen to the Spirit and understand what the Spirit is saying to the churches.

3:4
Jude 1:23

3:5
Exod 32:32-33
Ps 69:28
Matt 10:32
Luke 12:8
Rev 13:8; 17:8;
20:12

3:6
Rev 2:7

The Message to the Church in Philadelphia

7" Write this letter to the angel of the church in Philadelphia. This is the message from the one who is holy and true. He is the one who has the key of David. He opens doors, and no one can shut them; he shuts doors, and no one can open them.

3:7
Job 12:14
Isa 22:22
Matt 16:19

8" I know all the things you do, and I have opened a door for you that no one can shut. You have little strength, yet you obeyed my word and did not deny me. 9Look! I will force those who belong to Satan—those liars who say they are Jews but are not—to come and bow down at your feet. They will acknowledge that you are the ones I love.

3:8
Acts 14:27
Rev 2:13

3:9
Isa 43:4; 49:23
2 Cor 11:14-15
Rev 2:9

10" Because you have obeyed my command to persevere, I will protect you from the great time of testing that will come upon the whole world to test those who belong to this world. 11Look, I am coming quickly. Hold on to what you have, so that no one will take away your crown. 12All who are victorious will become pillars in the Temple of my God, and they will never have to leave it. And I will write my God's name on them, and they will be citizens in the city of my God—the new Jerusalem that comes down from heaven from my God. And they will have my new name inscribed upon them. 13Anyone who is willing to hear should listen to the Spirit and understand what the Spirit is saying to the churches.

3:10
2 Pet 2:9
Rev 2:10

3:11
Rev 2:25; 22:7,
12, 20

3:12
Ezek 48:35
Gal 4:26
Rev 21:2, 10

3:13
Rev 2:7

The Message to the Church in Laodicea

14" Write this letter to the angel of the church in Laodicea. This is the message from the one who is the Amen—the faithful and true witness, the ruler* of God's creation:

3:14
John 1:3
2 Cor 1:20
Col 1:15-18
Rev 1:5

15" I know all the things you do, that you are neither hot nor cold. I wish you were one or the other! 16But since you are like lukewarm water, I will spit you out of my mouth!

3:15
Rom 12:11

3:14 Or *the source.*

3:5 To be "clothed in white" means to be set apart for God and made pure. Christ promises future honor and eternal life to those who stand firm in their faith. The names of all believers are registered in the Book of Life. This book symbolizes God's knowledge of who belongs to him. All such people are guaranteed a listing in the Book of Life and are introduced to the hosts of heaven as belonging to Christ (see Luke 12:8, 9).

3:7 Philadelphia was founded by the citizens of Pergamum. The community was built in a frontier area as a gateway to the central plateau of Asia Minor. Philadelphia's residents kept barbarians out of the region and brought in Greek culture and language. The city was destroyed by an earthquake in A.D. 17, and aftershocks kept the people so worried that most of them lived outside the city limits.

3:7 The "key of David" represents Christ's authority to open the door into his future Kingdom. After the door is opened, no one can close it—salvation is assured. Once it is closed, no one can open it—judgment is certain.

• **3:10** Some believe that "I will protect you from the great time of testing" means there will be a future time of great tribulation from which true believers will be spared. Others interpret this to mean that the church will go through the time of tribulation and that God will keep them strong in the midst of it. Still others believe this refers to times of great distress in general, the church's suffering through the ages. Whatever the case, our emphasis should be on patiently obeying God no matter what we may face.

• **3:11** Christians have differing gifts, abilities, experience, and

maturity. God doesn't expect us all to be and act the same, but he does expect us to "hold on" to what we have, to persevere in using our resources for him. The Philadelphians are commended for their effort to obey (3:8) and encouraged to hold tightly to whatever strength they have. You may be a new believer and feel that your faith and spiritual strength are little. Use what you have to live for Christ, and God will commend you.

3:12 The new Jerusalem is the future dwelling of the people of God (21:2). We will have a new citizenship in God's future Kingdom. Everything will be new, pure, and secure.

3:15 Laodicea was the wealthiest of the seven cities, known for its banking industry, manufacture of wool, and a medical school that produced eye ointment. But the city had always had a problem with its water supply. At one time an aqueduct was built to bring water to the city from hot springs. But by the time the water reached the city, it was neither hot nor refreshingly cool—only lukewarm. The church had become as bland as the tepid water that came into the city.

• **3:15, 16** Lukewarm water makes a disgusting drink. The church in Laodicea had become lukewarm and thus distasteful and repugnant. The believers didn't take a stand for anything; indifference had led to idleness. By neglecting to do anything for Christ, the church had become hardened and self-satisfied, and it was destroying itself. There is nothing more disgusting than a half-hearted, nominal Christian who is self-sufficient. Don't settle for following God halfway. Let Christ fire up your faith and get you into the action.

3:17
Hos 12:8
Zech 11:5
1 Cor 4:8

3:19
Prov 3:12
1 Cor 11:32
Heb 12:6
Rev 2:5

3:20
John 14:23

3:21
Matt 19:28
Rev 5:5

3:22
Rev 2:7

¹⁷You say, 'I am rich. I have everything I want. I don't need a thing!' And you don't realize that you are wretched and miserable and poor and blind and naked. ¹⁸I advise you to buy gold from me—gold that has been purified by fire. Then you will be rich. And also buy white garments so you will not be shamed by your nakedness. And buy ointment for your eyes so you will be able to see. ¹⁹I am the one who corrects and disciplines everyone I love. Be diligent and turn from your indifference.

²⁰ "Look! Here I stand at the door and knock. If you hear me calling and open the door, I will come in, and we will share a meal as friends. ²¹I will invite everyone who is victorious to sit with me on my throne, just as I was victorious and sat with my Father on his throne. ²²Anyone who is willing to hear should listen to the Spirit and understand what the Spirit is saying to the churches."

B. MESSAGE FOR THE CHURCH (4:1—22:21)

Moving from the conditions within the churches in Asia to the future of the universal church, John sees the course of coming events in a way similar to Daniel and Ezekiel. Many of these passages contain clear spiritual teachings, but others seem beyond our ability to understand. The clear teaching of this book is that God will defeat all evil in the end. We must live in obedience to Jesus Christ, the coming Conqueror and Judge.

4:1
Exod 19:20, 24
Ezek 1:1
Dan 2:28-29, 45

4:2
Isa 6:1
Ezek 1:26-27

4:3
Ezek 1:26-28

1. Worshiping God in heaven

4 Then as I looked, I saw a door standing open in heaven, and the same voice I had heard before spoke to me with the sound of a mighty trumpet blast. The voice said, "Come up here, and I will show you what must happen after these things." ²And instantly I was in the Spirit,* and I saw a throne in heaven and someone sitting on it! ³The one sitting on the throne was as brilliant as gemstones—jasper and carnelian.

4:2 Or *in spirit.*

• **3:17** Some believers assume that numerous material possessions are a sign of God's spiritual blessing. Laodicea was a wealthy city, and the church was also wealthy. But what the Laodiceans could see and buy had become more valuable to them than what is unseen and eternal. Wealth, luxury, and ease can make people feel confident, satisfied, and complacent. But no matter how much you possess or how much money you make, you have nothing if you don't have a vital relationship with Christ. How does your current level of wealth affect your spiritual desire? Instead of centering your life primarily on comfort and luxury, find your true riches in Christ.

3:18 Laodicea was known for its great wealth; Christ told the Laodiceans to buy their gold from him (real spiritual treasures). The city was proud of its cloth and dyeing industries; Christ told them to purchase white garments from him (his righteousness). Laodicea prided itself on its precious eye ointment that healed many eye problems; Christ told them to get medicine from him to heal their eyes so they could see the truth (John 9:39). Christ was showing the Laodiceans that true value was not in material possessions but in a right relationship with God. Their possessions and achievements were valueless compared with the everlasting future of Christ's Kingdom.

• **3:19** God would discipline this lukewarm church unless it turned from its indifference toward him. God's purpose in discipline is not to punish but to bring people back to him. Are you lukewarm in your devotion to God? God may discipline you to help you out of your uncaring attitude, but he uses only loving discipline. You can avoid God's discipline by drawing near to him again through confession, service, worship, and studying his Word. Just as the spark of love can be rekindled in marriage, so the Holy Spirit can reignite our zeal for God when we allow him to work in our heart.

• **3:20** The Laodicean church was complacent and rich. They felt self-satisfied, but they didn't have Christ's presence among them. Christ knocked at the door of their hearts, but they were so busy enjoying worldly pleasures that they didn't notice that he was trying to enter. The pleasures of this world—money, security,

material possessions—can be dangerous, because their temporary satisfaction makes us indifferent to God's offer of lasting satisfaction. If you find yourself feeling indifferent to church, to God, or to the Bible, you have begun to shut God out of your life. Leave the door of your heart constantly open to God, and you won't need to worry about hearing his knock. Letting him in is your only hope for lasting fulfillment.

• **3:20** Jesus knocks at the door of our heart because he wants to save us and have fellowship with us. He is patient and persistent in trying to get through to us—not breaking and entering, but knocking. He allows us to decide whether or not to open our life to him. Do you intentionally keep his life-changing presence and power on the other side of the door?

• **3:22** At the end of each letter to these churches, the believers were urged to listen and understand what was written to them. Although a different message was addressed to each church, all the messages contain warnings and principles for everyone. Which letter speaks most directly to your church? Which has the greatest bearing on your own spiritual condition at this time? How will you respond?

4:1 Chapters 4 and 5 record glimpses into Christ's glory. Here we see into the throne room of heaven. God is on the throne and orchestrating all the events that John will record. The world is not spinning out of control; the God of creation will carry out his plans as Christ initiates the final battle with the forces of evil. John shows us heaven before showing us earth so that we will not be frightened by future events.

4:1 The voice John had first heard that sounded like a trumpet blast was the voice of Christ (see 1:10, 11).

4:2 Four times in the book of Revelation John says he was "in the Spirit" (1:10; 4:2; 17:3; 21:10). This expression means that the Holy Spirit was giving him a vision—showing him situations and events he could not have seen with mere human eyesight. All true prophecy comes from God through the Holy Spirit (2 Peter 1:20, 21).

And the glow of an emerald circled his throne like a rainbow. [4] Twenty-four thrones surrounded him, and twenty-four elders sat on them. They were all clothed in white and had gold crowns on their heads. [5] And from the throne came flashes of lightning and the rumble of thunder. And in front of the throne were seven lampstands with burning flames. They are the seven spirits* of God. [6] In front of the throne was a shiny sea of glass, sparkling like crystal.

In the center and around the throne were four living beings, each covered with eyes, front and back. [7] The first of these living beings had the form of a lion; the second looked like an ox; the third had a human face; and the fourth had the form of an eagle with wings spread out as though in flight. [8] Each of these living beings had six wings, and their wings were covered with eyes, inside and out. Day after day and night after night they keep on saying,

> "Holy, holy, holy is the Lord God Almighty—
>   the one who always was, who is, and who is still to come."

[9] Whenever the living beings give glory and honor and thanks to the one sitting on the throne, the one who lives forever and ever, [10] the twenty-four elders fall down and worship the one who lives forever and ever. And they lay their crowns before the throne and say,

> [11] "You are worthy, O Lord our God,
>   to receive glory and honor and power.
> For you created everything,
>   and it is for your pleasure that they exist and were created."

The Lamb Opens the Scroll

5 And I saw a scroll in the right hand of the one who was sitting on the throne. There was writing on the inside and the outside of the scroll, and it was sealed with seven seals. [2] And I saw a strong angel, who shouted with a loud voice: "Who is worthy to break the seals on this scroll and unroll it?" [3] But no one in heaven or on earth or under the earth was able to open the scroll and read it.

[4] Then I wept because no one could be found who was worthy to open the scroll and read it. [5] But one of the twenty-four elders said to me, "Stop weeping! Look, the Lion of

4:5 See 1:4 and 3:1, where the same expression is translated *the sevenfold Spirit.*

4:4
Isa 24:23
Rev 11:16; 19:4

4:5
Exod 19:16
Ezek 1:13
Zech 4:2
Rev 1:4; 5:6

4:6-7
Ezek 1:5-22; 10:12, 14
Rev 15:7; 19:4

4:8
Isa 6:2
Ezek 1:18; 10:12
Amos 3:13

4:9
Dan 4:34
Rev 4:2; 5:1

4:10
Rev 4:4; 5:8, 14

4:11
Rev 10:6

5:1
Isa 29:11
Ezek 2:9-10
Dan 12:4

5:3
Phil 2:10

5:5
Gen 49:9
Isa 11:1, 10
Heb 7:14

● **4:4** Who are these 24 elders? Because there were 12 tribes of Israel in the Old Testament and 12 apostles in the New Testament, the 24 elders in this vision probably represent all the redeemed of God for all time (both before and after Christ's death and resurrection). They symbolize all those—both Jews and Gentiles—who are now part of God's family. The 24 elders show us that *all* the redeemed of the Lord are worshiping him.

4:5 In Revelation, lightning and thunder are connected with significant events in heaven. They remind us of the lightning and thunder at Mount Sinai when God gave the people his laws (Exodus 19:16). The Old Testament often uses such imagery to reflect God's power and majesty (Psalm 77:18).

4:5 The "seven spirits" is another name for the Holy Spirit. See also Zechariah 4:2-6, where the seven lamps are equated with the one Spirit.

4:6 Glass was very rare in New Testament times, and crystal-clear glass was virtually impossible to find (see 1 Corinthians 13:12). The "sea of glass" highlights both the magnificence and holiness of God.

● **4:6, 7** Just as the Holy Spirit is seen symbolically in the seven lighted lamps, so the "four living beings" represent the attributes (the qualities and character) of God. These creatures were not real animals. Like the cherubim (the highest order of the angels), they guard God's throne, lead others in worship, and proclaim God's holiness. God's attributes symbolized in the animal-like appearance of these four creatures are majesty and power (the lion), faithfulness (the ox), intelligence (the human), and sover-

eignty (the eagle). The Old Testament prophet Ezekiel saw four similar creatures in one of his visions (Ezekiel 1:5-10).

● **4:11** The point of this chapter is summed up in this verse: All creatures in heaven and earth will praise and honor God because he is the creator and sustainer of everything.

5:1 In John's day, books were written on scrolls—pieces of papyrus or vellum up to 30 feet long, rolled up and sealed with clay or wax. The scroll that John sees contains the full account of what God has in store for the world. The seven seals indicate the importance of its contents. The seals are located throughout the scroll so that as each one is broken, more of the scroll can be read to reveal another phase of God's plan for the end of the world. Only Christ is worthy to break the seals and open the scroll (5:3-5).

5:1ff Chapter 5 continues the glimpse into heaven begun in chapter 4.

● **5:5** The Lion, Jesus, proved himself worthy to break the seals and open the scroll by living a perfect life of obedience to God, dying on the cross for the sins of the world, and rising from the dead to show his power and authority over evil and death. Only Christ conquered sin, death, hell, and Satan himself; so only he can be trusted with the world's future. "Heir to David's throne" refers to Jesus being from David's family line, thus fulfilling the promise of the Messiah in the Old Testament.

● **5:5, 6** Jesus Christ is pictured as both a Lion (symbolizing his authority and power) and a Lamb (symbolizing his submission to God's will). One of the elders calls John to look at the Lion, the tribe of Judah, the heir to David's throne,* has conquered. He is worthy to open the scroll and break its seven seals."

5:6
Isa 53:7
Zech 4:10
John 1:29, 36
Rev 1:4; 4:5
5:7
Rev 5:1
5:8
Rev 4:4, 6; 8:3-4;
14:2; 15:2

⁶I looked and I saw a Lamb that had been killed but was now standing between the throne and the four living beings and among the twenty-four elders. He had seven horns and seven eyes, which are the seven spirits* of God that are sent out into every part of the earth. ⁷He stepped forward and took the scroll from the right hand of the one sitting on the throne. ⁸And as he took the scroll, the four living beings and the twenty-four elders fell down before the Lamb. Each one had a harp, and they held gold bowls filled with incense—the prayers of God's people!

5:5 Greek *the root of David.*   **5:6** See note on 4:5.

EVENTS IN REVELATION DESCRIBED ELSEWHERE IN THE BIBLE	Other Reference	Revelation Reference	Event
	Ezekiel 1:22–28	4:2, 3; 10:1–3	Glowing rainbow around God's throne
	Isaiah 53:7	5:6–8	Christ is pictured as a Lamb
	Psalm 96	5:9–14	New song
	Zechariah 1:7–11; 6:1–8	6:1–8	Horses and riders
	Isaiah 2:19–22	6:12; 8:5; 11:13	Earthquake
	Joel 2:28–32; Acts 2:14–21	6:12	Moon turns blood red
	Mark 13:21–25	6:13	Stars falling from the sky
	Isaiah 34:1–4	6:14	Sky rolled up like a scroll
	Zephaniah 1:14–18; 1 Thessalonians 5:1–3	6:15–17	God's inescapable wrath
	Jeremiah 49:35–39	7:1	Four winds of judgment
	Luke 8:26–34	9:1, 2; 17:3–8	Bottomless pit
	Joel 1:2—2:11	9:3–11	Plague of locusts
	Luke 21:20–24	11:1, 2	Trampling of the holy city of Jerusalem
	Zechariah 4	11:3–6	Two olive trees as witnesses
	Daniel 7	13:1–10	A beast coming out of the sea
	2 Thessalonians 2:7–14	13:11–15	Wondrous signs and miracles done by the evil beast
	Jeremiah 25:15–29	14:9–12	Drinking the cup of God's wrath
	Isaiah 21:1–10	18:2, 3	"Babylon" falls
	Matthew 22:1–14	19:5–8	Wedding feast of the Lamb
	Ezekiel 38, 39	20:7–10	Conflict with Gog and Magog
	John 5:19–30	20:11–15	Judging of all people
	Ezekiel 37:21–28	21:3	God lives among his people
	Isaiah 25:1–8	21:4	Our tears will be wiped away forever
	Genesis 2:8–14	22:1, 2	Tree of life
	1 Corinthians 13:11, 12	22:3–5	We will see God face to face
	Daniel 7:18–28	22:5	Believers will reign with God forever

but when John looks he sees a Lamb. Christ the Lamb was the perfect sacrifice for the sins of all; therefore, only he can save us from the terrible events revealed by the scroll. Christ the Lamb won the greatest battle of all. He defeated all the forces of evil by dying on the cross. The role of Christ the Lion will be to lead the battle where Satan is finally defeated (19:19-21). Christ the Lion is victorious because of what Christ the Lamb has already done. We will participate in his victory, not because of our effort or goodness, but because he has promised eternal life to all who believe in him.

5:6 John says the Lamb "had been killed"; the wounds inflicted on Jesus' body during his trial and crucifixion could still be seen (see John 20:24-31). Jesus was called the Lamb of God by John

the Baptist (John 1:29). In the Old Testament, lambs were sacrificed to atone for sins; the Lamb of God died as the final sacrifice for all sins (see Isaiah 53:7; Hebrews 10:1-12, 18).

5:6 The horns symbolize strength and power (see 1 Kings 22:11; Zechariah 1:18). Although Christ is a sacrificial lamb, he is in no way weak. He was killed, but now he lives in God's strength and power. In Zechariah 4:2-10, the eyes are equated with the seven lamps and the one Spirit.

[9]And they sang a new song with these words:

"You are worthy to take the scroll
  and break its seals and open it.
For you were killed, and your blood has ransomed people for God
  from every tribe and language and people and nation.
[10] And you have caused them to become God's kingdom and his priests.
  And they will reign* on the earth."

[11]Then I looked again, and I heard the singing of thousands and millions of angels around the throne and the living beings and the elders. [12]And they sang in a mighty chorus:

"The Lamb is worthy—the Lamb who was killed.
  He is worthy to receive power and riches
  and wisdom and strength
  and honor and glory and blessing."

[13]And then I heard every creature in heaven and on earth and under the earth and in the sea. They also sang:

"Blessing and honor and glory and power
  belong to the one sitting on the throne
  and to the Lamb forever and ever."

[14]And the four living beings said, "Amen!" And the twenty-four elders fell down and worshiped God and the Lamb.

2. Opening the seven seals

The Lamb Breaks the First Six Seals

6 As I watched, the Lamb broke the first of the seven seals on the scroll. Then one of the four living beings called out with a voice that sounded like thunder, "Come!" [2]I looked up and saw a white horse. Its rider carried a bow, and a crown was placed on his head. He rode out to win many battles and gain the victory.

5:10 Some manuscripts read *they are reigning.*

5:9
Ps 144:9
Rev 14:3

5:10
Exod 19:6
1 Pet 2:5-9
Rev 1:6; 20:4

5:11
Dan 7:10
Heb 12:22
Rev 4:4, 6

5:12
1 Chr 29:11
Isa 53:7
John 1:29, 36
Rev 4:11

5:13
Phil 2:10
Rev 4:11; 5:7

5:14
Rev 4:6, 9-10

6:1
Rev 5:1, 6

6:2
Zech 1:8; 6:1-3
Rev 14:14;
19:11-12

• **5:9, 10** People from every nation are praising God before his throne. God's message of salvation and eternal life is not limited to a specific culture, race, or country. Anyone who comes to God in repentance and faith is accepted by him and will be part of his Kingdom. Don't allow prejudice or bias to keep you from sharing Christ with others. Christ welcomes all people into his Kingdom.

• **5:9, 10** The song of God's people praises Christ's work. He (1) was killed, (2) ransomed them with his blood, (3) gathered them into a Kingdom, (4) made them priests, and (5) appointed them to reign on the earth. Jesus has already died and paid the penalty for sin. He is now gathering us into his Kingdom and making us priests. In the future we will reign with him. Worship God and praise him for what he has done, what he is doing, and what he will do for all who trust in him. When we realize the glorious future that awaits us, we will find the strength to face our present difficulties.

• **5:10** The believers' song praises Christ for bringing them into the Kingdom and making them kings and priests. While now we are sometimes despised and mocked for our faith (John 15:17-27), in the future we will reign over all the earth (Luke 22:29, 30). Christ's death made all believers priests of God—the channels of blessing between God and people (1 Peter 2:5-9).

5:11 Angels are spiritual beings created by God who help carry out his work on earth. They bring messages (Luke 1:26-28), protect God's people (Daniel 6:22), offer encouragement (Genesis 16:7ff), give guidance (Exodus 14:19), bring punishment (2 Samuel 24:16), patrol the earth (Ezekiel 1:9-14), and fight the forces of evil (2 Kings 6:16-18; Revelation 20:1). There are both good and evil angels (12:7), but because evil angels are allied with Satan, they have considerably less power and authority than

good angels. Eventually, the main role of the good angels will be to offer continuous praise to God (see also 19:1-3).

5:14 The scene in chapter 5 shows us that only the Lamb, Jesus Christ, is worthy to open the scroll (the events of history). Jesus, not Satan, holds the future. Jesus Christ is in control, and he alone is worthy to set into motion the events of the last days of history.

• **6:1ff** This is the first of three seven-part judgments. The trumpets (chapters 8–9) and the bowls (chapter 16) are the other two. As each seal is opened, Christ the Lamb sets in motion events that will bring about the end of human history. This scroll is not completely opened until the seventh seal is broken (8:1). The contents of the scroll reveal humankind's depravity and portray God's authority over the events of human history.

6:2ff Four horses appear as the first four seals are opened. The horses represent God's judgment of people's sin and rebellion. God is directing human history—even using his enemies to accomplish his purposes. The four horses are a foretaste of the final judgments yet to come. Some view this chapter as a parallel to the Olivet Discourse (see Matthew 24). The imagery of four horses is also found in Zechariah 6:1-8.

• **6:2-8** Each of the four horses is a different color. Some assume that the white horse represents victory and that its rider must be Christ (because Christ later rides to victory on a white horse—19:11). But because the other three horses relate to judgment and destruction, this rider on a white horse would most likely not be Christ. The four are part of the unfolding judgment of God, and it would be premature for Christ to ride forth as conqueror. The other horses represent different kinds of judgment: red for warfare and bloodshed; black for famine; pale green for death. The high prices of wheat and barley illustrate famine conditions. But the worst is yet to come.

6:4
Zech 1:8; 6:2
Matt 10:34

6:5
Zech 6:2, 6

6:8
Jer 14:12; 15:2-3
Hos 13:14
Rev 1:18; 20:13

6:9
Exod 29:12
Lev 4:7
Rev 14:18; 20:4

6:10
Ps 79:10
Zech 1:12
Luke 18:7
Rev 3:7, 10; 19:2

6:11
Heb 11:40
Rev 3:4

6:12
Joel 2:10
Matt 24:29
Rev 16:18

6:13
Isa 34:4
Rev 8:10; 9:1

6:14
Ps 46:2
2 Pet 3:10
Rev 16:20; 20:11;
21:1

6:15
Isa 2:10, 19, 21
Jer 4:29

6:16
Hos 10:8
Luke 23:30

6:17
Joel 2:11
Zeph 1:14-15
Mal 3:2

³When the Lamb broke the second seal, I heard the second living being say, "Come!" ⁴And another horse appeared, a red one. Its rider was given a mighty sword and the authority to remove peace from the earth. And there was war and slaughter everywhere.

⁵When the Lamb broke the third seal, I heard the third living being say, "Come!" And I looked up and saw a black horse, and its rider was holding a pair of scales in his hand. ⁶And a voice from among the four living beings said, "A loaf of wheat bread or three loaves of barley for a day's pay.* And don't waste* the olive oil and wine."

⁷And when the Lamb broke the fourth seal, I heard the fourth living being say, "Come!" ⁸And I looked up and saw a horse whose color was pale green like a corpse. And Death was the name of its rider, who was followed around by the Grave.* They were given authority over one-fourth of the earth, to kill with the sword and famine and disease* and wild animals.

⁹And when the Lamb broke the fifth seal, I saw under the altar the souls of all who had been martyred for the word of God and for being faithful in their witness. ¹⁰They called loudly to the Lord and said, "O Sovereign Lord, holy and true, how long will it be before you judge the people who belong to this world for what they have done to us? When will you avenge our blood against these people?" ¹¹Then a white robe was given to each of them. And they were told to rest a little longer until the full number of their brothers and sisters*—their fellow servants of Jesus—had been martyred.

¹²I watched as the Lamb broke the sixth seal, and there was a great earthquake. The sun became as dark as black cloth, and the moon became as red as blood. ¹³Then the stars of the sky fell to the earth like green figs falling from trees shaken by mighty winds. ¹⁴And the sky was rolled up like a scroll and taken away. And all of the mountains and all of the islands disappeared. ¹⁵Then the kings of the earth, the rulers, the generals, the wealthy people, the people with great power, and every slave and every free person—all hid themselves in the caves and among the rocks of the mountains. ¹⁶And they cried to the mountains and the rocks, "Fall on us and hide us from the face of the one who sits on the throne and from the wrath of the Lamb. ¹⁷For the great day of their wrath has come, and who will be able to survive?"

6:6a Greek *A choinix of wheat for a denarius, and 3 choinix of barley for a denarius.*   **6:6b** Or *hurt.*   **6:8a** Greek *by Hades.*   **6:8b** Greek *death.*   **6:11** Greek *their brothers.*

6:8 It is not clear whether "the Grave" was on a separate horse than Death or merely rode along with Death, but the riders described in verses 2-8 are commonly referred to as the four horsemen of the Apocalypse.

6:8 The four riders are given power over one-fourth of the earth, indicating that God is still limiting his judgment—it is not yet complete. With these judgments there is still time for unbelievers to turn to Christ and away from their sin. In this case, the limited punishment not only demonstrates God's wrath on sin but also his merciful love in giving people yet another opportunity to turn to him before he brings final judgment.

• **6:9** The altar represents the altar of sacrifice in the Temple, where animals were sacrificed to atone for sins. Instead of the animals' blood at the base of the altar, John saw the souls of martyrs who had died for preaching the Good News. These martyrs were told that still more would lose their lives for their belief in Christ (6:11). In the face of warfare, famine, persecution, and death, Christians will be called on to stand firmly for what they believe. Only those who endure to the end will be rewarded by God (Mark 13:13).

• **6:9-11** The martyrs are eager for God to bring justice to the earth, but they are told to wait. God is not waiting until a certain number is reached, but he is promising that those who suffer and die for their faith will not be forgotten. Rather, they will be singled out by God for special honor. We may wish for justice immediately, as these martyrs did, but we must be patient. God works according to his own timetable, and he promises justice. No suffering for the sake of God's Kingdom, however, is wasted.

6:12 The sixth seal changes the scene back to the physical world. The first five judgments were directed toward specific areas, but this judgment is universal. Everyone will be afraid when the earth itself trembles.

• **6:15-17** At the sight of God sitting on the throne, all human beings, great and small, will be terrified, calling for the mountains to fall on them so that they will not have to face the judgment of the Lamb. This vivid picture was not intended to frighten believers. For them, the Lamb is a gentle Savior. But those kings, rulers, and generals and other powerful people who previously showed no fear of God and arrogantly flaunted their unbelief will find that they were wrong, and in that day they will have to face God's wrath. No one who has rejected God can survive the day of his wrath, but those who belong to Christ will receive a reward rather than punishment. Do you belong to Christ? If so, you need not fear these final days.

God's People Will Be Preserved

7 Then I saw four angels standing at the four corners of the earth, holding back the four winds from blowing upon the earth. Not a leaf rustled in the trees, and the sea became as smooth as glass. ²And I saw another angel coming from the east, carrying the seal of the living God. And he shouted out to those four angels who had been given power to injure land and sea, ³"Wait! Don't hurt the land or the sea or the trees until we have placed the seal of God on the foreheads of his servants."

⁴And I heard how many were marked with the seal of God. There were 144,000 who were sealed from all the tribes of Israel:

⁵ from Judah	12,000
from Reuben	12,000
from Gad	12,000
⁶ from Asher	12,000
from Naphtali	12,000
from Manasseh	12,000
⁷ from Simeon	12,000
from Levi	12,000
from Issachar	12,000
⁸ from Zebulun	12,000
from Joseph	12,000
from Benjamin	12,000

Praise from the Great Multitude

⁹After this I saw a vast crowd, too great to count, from every nation and tribe and people and language, standing in front of the throne and before the Lamb. They were clothed in white and held palm branches in their hands. ¹⁰And they were shouting with a mighty shout, "Salvation comes from our God on the throne and from the Lamb!"

¹¹And all the angels were standing around the throne and around the elders and the four living beings. And they fell face down before the throne and worshiped God. ¹²They said,

---

7:1ff The sixth seal has been opened, and the people of the earth have tried to hide from God, saying, "Who will be able to survive?" (6:12-17). Just when all hope seems lost, four angels hold back the four winds of judgment until God's people are sealed as his own. Only then will God open the seventh seal (8:1).

7:2 A seal on a scroll or document identified and protected its contents. God places his own seal on his followers, identifying them as his own and guaranteeing his protection over their souls. This shows how valuable we are to him. Our physical bodies may be beaten, maimed, or even destroyed, but *nothing* can harm our souls when we have been sealed by God. See Ephesians 1:13 for the seal of the Holy Spirit.

7:3 God's seal is placed on the foreheads of his servants. This seal is the exact opposite of the mark of the beast explained in 13:16. These two marks place the people in two distinct categories—those owned by God and those owned by Satan.

7:4-8 The number 144,000 is 12 x 12 x 1,000, symbolizing completeness—all God's followers will be brought safely to him; not one will be overlooked or forgotten. God seals these believers either by withdrawing them from the earth (this is called the Rapture) or by giving them special strength and courage to make it through this time of great persecution. Even though many believers have to undergo persecution, the seal does not necessarily guarantee protection from physical harm—many will die (see 6:11)—but God will protect them from spiritual harm. No matter what happens, they will be brought to their reward of eternal life. Their destiny is secure. These believers will not fall away from God even though they may undergo intense persecution.

This is not saying that 144,000 individuals must be sealed before the persecution comes, but that when persecution begins, the faithful will have already been sealed (marked by God), and they will remain true to him until the end.

7:4-8 This is a different list from the usual listing of the 12 tribes in the Old Testament, because it is a symbolic list of God's true followers. (1) Judah is mentioned first because Judah is both the tribe of David and of Jesus the Messiah (Genesis 49:8-12; Matthew 1:1). (2) Levi had no tribal allotment because of the Levites' work for God in the Temple (Deuteronomy 18:1), but here the tribe is given a place as a reward for faithfulness. (3) Dan is not mentioned because it was known for rebellion and idolatry, traits unacceptable for God's followers (Genesis 49:17). (4) The two tribes representing Joseph (usually called Ephraim and Manasseh, after Joseph's sons) are here called Joseph and Manasseh because of Ephraim's rebellion. See Genesis 49 for the story of the beginning of these 12 tribes.

7:9 Who is this vast crowd? While some interpreters identify it as the martyrs described in 6:9, it may also be the same group as the 144,000 just mentioned (7:4-8). The 144,000 were sealed by God before the great time of persecution; the vast crowd was brought to eternal life, as God had promised. Before, they were being prepared; now, they are victorious. This crowd in heaven is composed of all those who remained faithful to God throughout the generations. No true believer ever need worry about which group he or she will be in. God includes and protects each of us, and we are guaranteed a place in his presence.

7:10 People try many methods to remove the guilt of sin—good deeds, intellectual pursuits, and even casting blame on others. The crowd in heaven however, praises God, saying that salvation comes from him and from the Lamb. Salvation from sin's penalty can come only through Jesus Christ. Have you had the guilt of sin removed in the only way possible?

7:11 More information about the elders is found in the note on 4:4. The four living beings are explained further in the note on 4:6, 7.

7:12
Rev 5:12-14

"Amen! Blessing and glory and wisdom
and thanksgiving and honor and power and strength
belong to our God forever and forever. Amen!"

7:13
Rev 6:11; 7:9

¹³Then one of the twenty-four elders asked me, "Who are these who are clothed in

7:14
Dan 12:1
Rev 6:11; 22:14

white? Where do they come from?"

¹⁴And I said to him, "Sir, you are the one who knows."

7:15
Rev 4:9; 11:19;
22:3

Then he said to me, "These are the ones coming out of the great tribulation. They
washed their robes in the blood of the Lamb and made them white. ¹⁵That is why they

7:16
Isa 49:10

are standing in front of the throne of God, serving him day and night in his Temple. And
he who sits on the throne will live among them and shelter them. ¹⁶They will never again

7:17
Ps 23:1-5
Isa 25:8; 49:10
John 10:11, 14
Rev 21:4, 6; 22:1

be hungry or thirsty, and they will be fully protected from the scorching noontime heat.
¹⁷For the Lamb who stands in front of the throne will be their Shepherd. He will lead
them to the springs of life-giving water. And God will wipe away all their tears."

8:1
Rev 6:1-17

The Lamb Breaks the Seventh Seal

8:2
Rev 9:1, 13; 1:15

8 When the Lamb broke the seventh seal, there was silence throughout heaven for
about half an hour. ²And I saw the seven angels who stand before God, and they
were given seven trumpets.

8:3
Exod 30:1-3
Rev 9:13

³Then another angel with a gold incense burner came and stood at the altar. And a
great quantity of incense was given to him to mix with the prayers of God's people, to

8:4
Ps 141:2
Rev 5:8; 8:3

be offered on the gold altar before the throne. ⁴The smoke of the incense, mixed with
the prayers of the saints, ascended up to God from the altar where the angel had poured

8:5
Exod 19:16-19
Lev 16:12
Rev 4:5; 11:19;
16:18

them out. ⁵Then the angel filled the incense burner with fire from the altar and threw it
down upon the earth; and thunder crashed, lightning flashed, and there was a terrible
earthquake.

3. Sounding the seven trumpets

The First Four Trumpets

8:7
Ezek 38:22
Joel 3:3
Zech 13:9

⁶Then the seven angels with the seven trumpets prepared to blow their mighty blasts.

⁷The first angel blew his trumpet, and hail and fire mixed with blood were thrown
down upon the earth, and one-third of the earth was set on fire. One-third of the trees

8:8
Jer 51:25
Zech 13:9

were burned, and all the grass was burned.

⁸Then the second angel blew his trumpet, and a great mountain of fire was thrown into

8:10
Isa 14:12
Rev 6:13; 9:1; 16:4

the sea. And one-third of the water in the sea became blood. ⁹And one-third of all things
living in the sea died. And one-third of all the ships on the sea were destroyed.

8:11
Jer 9:15

¹⁰Then the third angel blew his trumpet, and a great flaming star fell out of the sky,
burning like a torch. It fell upon one-third of the rivers and on the springs of water. ¹¹The

---

• **7:14** "The great tribulation" has been explained in several ways. Some believe it refers to the suffering of believers through the ages; others believe that there is a specific time of intense tribulation yet to come. In either case, these believers come through their times of suffering by remaining loyal to God. Because they remain faithful, God will give them eternal life with him (7:17).

• **7:14** It is difficult to imagine how blood could make any cloth white, but the blood of Jesus Christ is the world's greatest purifier because it removes the stain of sin. White symbolizes sinless perfection or holiness, which can be given to people only by the death of the sinless Lamb of God on our behalf. This is a picture of how we are saved through faith (see Isaiah 1:18; Romans 3:21-26).

• **7:16, 17** God will provide for his children's needs in their eternal home where there will be no hunger, thirst, or pain, and he will wipe away all tears. When you are suffering or torn apart by sorrow, take comfort in this promise of complete protection and relief.

• **7:17** In verses 1-8 we see the believers receiving a seal to protect them through a time of great tribulation and suffering; in verses 9-17 we see the believers finally with God in heaven. All who have been faithful through the ages are singing before God's

throne. Their tribulations and sorrows are over: no more tears for sin, for all sins are forgiven; no more tears for suffering, for all suffering is over; no more tears for death, for all believers have been resurrected to die no more.

8:1, 2 When the seventh seal is opened, the seven trumpet judgments are revealed. In the same way, the seventh trumpet will announce the seven bowl judgments in 11:15 and 16:1-21. The trumpet judgments, like the seal judgments, are only partial. God's final and complete judgment has not yet come.

8:3 An incense burner filled with live coals was used in Temple worship. Incense was poured on the coals, and the sweet-smelling smoke drifted upward, symbolizing believers' prayers ascending to God (see Exodus 30:7-9).

• **8:6** The trumpet blasts have three purposes: (1) to warn that judgment is certain, (2) to call the forces of good and evil to battle, and (3) to announce the return of the King, the Messiah. These warnings urge us to make sure our faith is firmly fixed on Christ.

• **8:7-12** Since only one-third of the earth is destroyed by these trumpet judgments, this is only a partial judgment from God. His full wrath is yet to be unleashed.

name of the star was Bitterness.* It made one-third of the water bitter, and many people died because the water was so bitter.

¹²Then the fourth angel blew his trumpet, and one-third of the sun was struck, and one-third of the moon, and one-third of the stars, and they became dark. And one-third of the day was dark and one-third of the night also.

¹³Then I looked up. And I heard a single eagle crying loudly as it flew through the air, "Terror, terror, terror to all who belong to this world because of what will happen when the last three angels blow their trumpets."

8:12
Exod 10:21
Ezek 32:7-8
Rev 6:12-13

8:13
Rev 3:10; 9:12

The Fifth Trumpet Brings the First Terror

9 Then the fifth angel blew his trumpet, and I saw a star that had fallen to earth from the sky, and he was given the key to the shaft of the bottomless pit. ²When he opened it, smoke poured out as though from a huge furnace, and the sunlight and air were darkened by the smoke.

³Then locusts came from the smoke and descended on the earth, and they were given power to sting like scorpions. ⁴They were told not to hurt the grass or plants or trees but to attack all the people who did not have the seal of God on their foreheads. ⁵They were told not to kill them but to torture them for five months with agony like the pain of scorpion stings. ⁶In those days people will seek death but will not find it. They will long to die, but death will flee away!

⁷The locusts looked like horses armed for battle. They had gold crowns on their heads, and they had human faces. ⁸Their hair was long like the hair of a woman, and their teeth were like the teeth of a lion. ⁹They wore armor made of iron, and their wings roared like an army of chariots rushing into battle. ¹⁰They had tails that stung like scorpions, with power to torture people. This power was given to them for five months. ¹¹Their king is the angel from the bottomless pit; his name in Hebrew is *Abaddon*, and in Greek, *Apollyon*—the Destroyer.

¹²The first terror is past, but look, two more terrors are coming!

9:1
Isa 14:12
Luke 8:31; 10:18

9:3
Rev 9:5, 10

9:4
Ezek 9:4, 6
Rev 7:3

9:6
Job 3:21
Rev 6:16

9:7
Joel 2:4-5

9:8
Joel 1:6

9:9
Joel 2:5

9:11
Job 26:6; 28:22

The Sixth Trumpet Brings the Second Terror

¹³Then the sixth angel blew his trumpet, and I heard a voice speaking from the four horns of the gold altar that stands in the presence of God. ¹⁴And the voice spoke to the sixth angel

9:14
Gen 15:18

8:11 Greek *Wormwood.*

• **8:13** Habakkuk used the image of an eagle to symbolize swiftness and destruction (see Habakkuk 1:8). The picture here is also of an eagle flying over all the earth, warning of the terrors yet to come. While both believers and unbelievers experience the terrors described in verses 7-12, those "who belong to this world" are the unbelievers who will meet spiritual harm through the next three trumpet judgments. God has guaranteed believers protection from spiritual harm (7:2, 3).

• **8:13** In 6:10, the martyrs call out to God, "How long will it be before you judge the people who belong to this world for what they have done to us? When will you avenge our blood against these people?" As we see the world's wickedness, we, too, may cry out to God, "How long?" In the following chapters, the judgment comes at last. We may be distressed and impatient, but God has his plan and his timing, and we must learn to trust him to know what is best. Judgment is coming—be sure of that. Thank God for the time he has given you to turn from sin. Use the available time to work to help others turn to him.

9:1 It is not known whether this "star" that fell from the sky is Satan, a fallen angel, Christ, or a good angel. Most likely it is a good angel, because the key to the shaft of the bottomless pit is normally held by Christ (1:17, 18), and it was temporarily given to this other being from heaven (see also 20:1). This being, whoever he may be, is still under God's control and authority. The bottomless pit represents the place of the demons and of Satan, the king of demons (9:11). See also Luke 8:31 for another reference to the bottomless pit.

9:3 The prophet Joel described a locust plague as a foreshadowing of the "day of the LORD," meaning God's coming

judgment (Joel 2:1-10). In the Old Testament, locusts were symbols of destruction because they destroyed vegetation. Here, however, they symbolize an invasion of demons called to torture people who do not believe in God. The limitations placed on the demons (they could only torment people for five months) show that they are under God's authority.

9:3ff Most likely these locusts are demons—evil spirits ruled by Satan who tempt people to sin. They were not created by Satan, because God is the Creator of all; rather, they are fallen angels who joined Satan in his rebellion. God limits what they can do; they can do nothing without his permission. Their main purpose on earth is to prevent, distort, or destroy people's relationship with God. Because they are corrupt and degenerate, their appearance reflects the distortion of their spirits. While it is important to recognize their evil activity so we can stay away from them, we must avoid any curiosity about or involvement with demonic forces or with the occult.

9:11 The locust-demons have a leader whose name in Hebrew and in Greek means "Destroyer." It may be a play on words by John to show that those who worshiped the great god Apollo worshiped only a demon.

9:13 The altar in the Temple had four projections, one at each corner, and these were called the horns of the altar (see Exodus 27:2).

9:14 The word *angels* here means fallen angels or demons. These four unidentified demons will be exceedingly evil and destructive. But note that they do not have the power to release themselves and do their evil work on earth. Instead, they are held back by God and will be released at a specific time, doing only what he allows them to do.

9:15
Rev 8:7-12; 9:18;
20:7

9:16
Rev 5:11; 7:4

9:17
Job 41:10-12

9:20
Deut 4:28; 32:17
Ps 115:4-7
Dan 5:23
Mic 5:13
Acts 7:41
1 Cor 10:19-20
Rev 2:21

9:21
Rev 16:9, 11, 21

10:1
Matt 17:2

10:3
Ps 29:3-9

10:4
Dan 8:26; 12:4, 9
Rev 22:10

10:5
Deut 32:40
Dan 12:7

10:6
Gen 14:19, 22
Exod 20:11
Neh 9:6
Ps 146:6

10:7
Dan 9:6, 10
Amos 3:7
Rev 11:15

10:9
Jer 15:16
Ezek 2:8–3:3

who held the trumpet: "Release the four angels who are bound at the great Euphrates River." ¹⁵And the four angels who had been prepared for this hour and day and month and year were turned loose to kill one-third of all the people on earth. ¹⁶They led an army of 200 million mounted troops—I heard an announcement of how many there were.

¹⁷And in my vision, I saw the horses and the riders sitting on them. The riders wore armor that was fiery red and sky blue and yellow. The horses' heads were like the heads of lions, and fire and smoke and burning sulfur billowed from their mouths. ¹⁸One-third of all the people on earth were killed by these three plagues—by the fire and the smoke and burning sulfur that came from the mouths of the horses. ¹⁹Their power was in their mouths, but also in their tails. For their tails had heads like snakes, with the power to injure people.

²⁰But the people who did not die in these plagues still refused to turn from their evil deeds. They continued to worship demons and idols made of gold, silver, bronze, stone, and wood—idols that neither see nor hear nor walk! ²¹And they did not repent of their murders or their witchcraft or their immorality or their thefts.

The Angel and the Small Scroll

10 Then I saw another mighty angel coming down from heaven, surrounded by a cloud, with a rainbow over his head. His face shone like the sun, and his feet were like pillars of fire. ²And in his hand was a small scroll, which he had unrolled. He stood with his right foot on the sea and his left foot on the land. ³And he gave a great shout, like the roar of a lion. And when he shouted, the seven thunders answered.

⁴When the seven thunders spoke, I was about to write. But a voice from heaven called to me: "Keep secret what the seven thunders said. Do not write it down."

⁵Then the mighty angel standing on the sea and on the land lifted his right hand to heaven. ⁶And he swore an oath in the name of the one who lives forever and ever, who created heaven and everything in it, the earth and everything in it, and the sea and everything in it. He said, "God will wait no longer. ⁷But when the seventh angel blows his trumpet, God's mysterious plan will be fulfilled. It will happen just as he announced it to his servants the prophets."

⁸Then the voice from heaven called to me again: "Go and take the unrolled scroll from the angel who is standing on the sea and on the land."

⁹So I approached him and asked him to give me the little scroll. "Yes, take it and eat it," he said. "At first it will taste like honey, but when you swallow it, it will make your

---

9:15 Here one-third of all people are killed. In 6:7, 8, one-fourth of all people were killed. Thus, over one-half of the people in the world will have been killed by God's great judgments. Even more would have been killed if God had not set limits on the destruction.

9:16 In John's day, this number of mounted troops in an army was inconceivable, but today there are countries and alliances that could easily amass this many soldiers. This huge army, led by the four demons, will be sent out to destroy one-third of the earth's population. But the judgment is still not complete.

• **9:20, 21** These people were so hard-hearted that even plagues did not drive them to God. People don't usually fall into immorality and evil suddenly—they slip into it a little bit at a time until, hardly realizing what has happened, they are irrevocably mired in their wicked ways. Any person who allows sin to take root in his or her life will end up in this predicament. Temptation entertained today becomes sin tomorrow, a habit the next day, then death and separation from God forever (see James 1:15). To think you could never become this evil is the first step toward a hard heart. Acknowledge your need to confess your sin before God.

10:1-6 The purpose of this mighty angel is clear—to announce the final judgments on the earth. His right foot on the sea and left foot on the land (10:2) indicate that his words deal with all creation, not just a limited part as did the seal and trumpet judgments. The seventh trumpet (11:15) will usher in the seven bowl judgments, which will bring an end to the present world. When this universal judgment comes, God's truth will prevail.

10:2 We see two scrolls in Revelation. The first contains a revelation of judgments against evil (5:1ff). The contents of the second small scroll are not indicated, but it also may contain a revelation of judgment.

• **10:4** Throughout history people have wanted to know what would happen in the future, and God reveals some of it in this book. But John was stopped from revealing certain parts of his vision. An angel also told the prophet Daniel that some visions he saw were not to be revealed yet to everyone (Daniel 12:9), and Jesus told his disciples that the time of the end is known by no one but God (Mark 13:32, 33). God has revealed all we need to know to live for him now. In our desire to be ready for the end, we must not place more emphasis on speculation about the last days than on living for God while we wait.

10:7 When God's plan for human history is completely revealed, all prophecy will be fulfilled. The end of the age will have arrived (see 11:15 and Ephesians 1:9, 10).

10:9, 10 The prophet Ezekiel had a vision in which he was told to eat a scroll filled with judgments against the nation of Israel (Ezekiel 3:1ff). The taste was sweet in his mouth, but the scroll's contents brought destruction—just like the scroll John was told to eat. God's Word is sweet to us as believers because it brings encouragement, but it sours our stomach because of the coming judgment we must pronounce on unbelievers.

stomach sour!" ¹⁰So I took the little scroll from the hands of the angel, and I ate it! It was sweet in my mouth, but it made my stomach sour. ¹¹Then he said to me, "You must prophesy again about many peoples, nations, languages, and kings."

10:11
Jer 1:10; 25:30
Dan 3:4
Rev 5:9

The Two Witnesses

11 Then I was given a measuring stick, and I was told, "Go and measure the Temple of God and the altar, and count the number of worshipers. ²But do not measure the outer courtyard, for it has been turned over to the nations. They will trample the holy city for 42 months. ³And I will give power to my two witnesses, and they will be clothed in sackcloth and will prophesy during those 1,260 days."

11:1
Ezek 40:3
Rev 21:15

11:2
Ezek 40:17-20
Luke 21:24
Rev 12:6; 13:5

⁴These two prophets are the two olive trees and the two lampstands that stand before the Lord of all the earth. ⁵If anyone tries to harm them, fire flashes from the mouths of the prophets and consumes their enemies. This is how anyone who tries to harm them must die. ⁶They have power to shut the skies so that no rain will fall for as long as they prophesy. And they have the power to turn the rivers and oceans into blood, and to send every kind of plague upon the earth as often as they wish.

11:3
Rev 2:13

11:4
Zech 4:3, 11, 14

11:5
2 Sam 22:9
2 Kgs 1:10
Jer 5:14

11:6
Exod 7:17-20
1 Kgs 17:1

⁷When they complete their testimony, the beast that comes up out of the bottomless pit will declare war against them. He will conquer them and kill them. ⁸And their bodies will lie in the main street of Jerusalem,* the city which is called "Sodom" and "Egypt," the city where their Lord was crucified. ⁹And for three and a half days, all peoples, tribes, languages, and nations will come to stare at their bodies. No one will be allowed to bury them. ¹⁰All the people who belong to this world will give presents to each other to celebrate the death of the two prophets who had tormented them.

11:7
Dan 7:21
Rev 13:1, 7

11:8
Isa 1:9-10
Rev 16:19

11:9
Ps 79:2-3

¹¹But after three and a half days, the spirit of life from God entered them, and they stood up! And terror struck all who were staring at them. ¹²Then a loud voice shouted from heaven, "Come up here!" And they rose to heaven in a cloud as their enemies watched.

11:10
Neh 8:10, 12

11:11
Ezek 37:5, 10

¹³And in the same hour there was a terrible earthquake that destroyed a tenth of the city. Seven thousand people died in that earthquake. And everyone who did not die was terrified and gave glory to the God of heaven.

11:12
2 Kgs 2:11
Acts 1:9
Rev 4:1

¹⁴The second terror is past, but look, now the third terror is coming quickly.

11:8 Greek *the great city.*

11:13
Ezek 38:19-20
Rev 16:9, 11

11:1ff This Temple is most likely a symbol of the church (all true believers), because there will be no Temple in the new Jerusalem (21:22). John measured the Temple to show that God is building walls of protection around his people to spare them from spiritual harm, and that there is a place reserved for all believers who remain faithful to God.

11:2 Those worshiping inside the Temple will be protected spiritually, but those outside will face great suffering. This is a way of saying that true believers will be protected through persecution, but those who refuse to believe will be destroyed.

• **11:3** These two witnesses bear strong resemblance to Moses and Elijah, two of God's mighty prophets. With God's power, Moses called plagues down upon the nation of Egypt (see Exodus 7–11). Elijah defeated the prophets of Baal (1 Kings 18). Both of these men appeared with Christ at his transfiguration (see Matthew 17:1-7).

• **11:3** In the book of Revelation, numbers are likely to have symbolic rather than literal meanings. The 42 months or 1,260 days equal 3½ years. As half of the perfect number 7, 3½ can indicate incompletion, imperfection, or even evil. Notice the

events predicted for this time period: there is trouble (Daniel 12:7), the holy city is trampled (11:2), the woman takes refuge in the wilderness (12:6), and the Devil-inspired beast exercises his authority (13:5). Some commentators link the 3½ years with the period of famine in the days of Elijah (Luke 4:25; James 5:17). Since Malachi predicted the return of Elijah before the Last Judgment (Malachi 4:5), and since the events in Daniel and Revelation pave the way for the Second Coming, perhaps John was making this connection. It is possible, of course, that the 3½ years are literal. If so, we will clearly recognize when the 3½ years are over! Whether symbolic or literal, however, they indicate that evil's reign will have a definite end.

11:7 This beast could be Satan or an agent of Satan.

11:8, 9 Jerusalem, once the great city and the capital of Israel, is now enemy territory. It is compared with Sodom and with Egypt, both well known for their evil. By the time of John's writing, Jerusalem had been destroyed by the Romans in 70 A.D., nearly a million Jews had been slaughtered, and the Temple treasures had been carried off to Rome.

• **11:10** The whole world rejoices at the deaths of these two witnesses, who have caused trouble by saying what the people didn't want to hear—words about their sin, their need for repentance, and the coming punishment. Sinful people hate those who call attention to their sin and who urge them to repent. They hated Christ, and they hate his followers (1 John 3:13). When you obey Christ and take a stand against sin, be prepared to experience the world's hatred. But remember that the great reward awaiting you in heaven far outweighs any suffering that you face now.

The Seventh Trumpet Brings the Third Terror

11:15
Ps 10:16
Dan 2:44; 7:14, 27
Rev 10:7; 12:10;
16:17

15Then the seventh angel blew his trumpet, and there were loud voices shouting in heaven: "The whole world has now become the kingdom of our Lord and of his Christ, and he will reign forever and ever."

11:16
Rev 4:4, 10

16And the twenty-four elders sitting on their thrones before God fell on their faces and worshiped him. 17And they said,

11:17
Amos 3:13; 4:13
Rev 1:8; 19:6

"We give thanks to you, Lord God Almighty,
the one who is and who always was,
for now you have assumed your great power
and have begun to reign.

11:18
Ps 2:1
Rev 10:7; 19:5;
20:12

18 The nations were angry with you,
but now the time of your wrath has come.
It is time to judge the dead and reward your servants.
You will reward your prophets and your holy people,
all who fear your name, from the least to the greatest.
And you will destroy all who have caused destruction on the earth."

11:19
2 Chr 5:7
Rev 4:5; 15:5

19Then, in heaven, the Temple of God was opened and the Ark of his covenant could be seen inside the Temple. Lightning flashed, thunder crashed and roared; there was a great hailstorm, and the world was shaken by a mighty earthquake.

4. Observing the great conflict

The Woman and the Dragon

12:2
Isa 26:17; 66:6-9
Mic 4:10

12 Then I witnessed in heaven an event of great significance. I saw a woman clothed with the sun, with the moon beneath her feet, and a crown of twelve stars on her head. 2She was pregnant, and she cried out in the pain of labor as she awaited her delivery.

12:3
Dan 7:7, 24
Rev 13:1; 17:3, 7,
12, 16

3Suddenly, I witnessed in heaven another significant event. I saw a large red dragon with seven heads and ten horns, with seven crowns on his heads. 4His tail dragged down one-third of the stars, which he threw to the earth. He stood before the woman as she was about to give birth to her child, ready to devour the baby as soon as it was born.

12:4
Dan 8:10

12:5
Ps 2:9
Rev 2:27; 19:15

5She gave birth to a boy who was to rule all nations with an iron rod. And the child was snatched away from the dragon and was caught up to God and to his throne. 6And the woman fled into the wilderness, where God had prepared a place to give her care for 1,260 days.

12:6
Rev 11:2; 13:5

11:15 The seventh trumpet is sounded, announcing the arrival of the King. There is now no turning back. The coming judgments are no longer partial but complete in their destruction. God is in control, and he unleashes his full wrath on the evil world that refuses to turn to him (9:20, 21). When his wrath begins, there will be no escape.

11:16 For more on the 24 elders, see the note on 4:4.

• **11:18** In the Bible, God gives rewards to his people according to what they deserve. Throughout the Old Testament, obedience often brought reward in this life (Deuteronomy 28), but obedience and immediate reward are not always linked. If they were, good people would always be rich, and suffering would always be a sign of sin. If we were quickly rewarded for every faithful deed, we would soon think we were pretty good. Before long, we would be doing many good deeds for purely selfish reasons. While it is true that God will reward us for our earthly deeds (see 20:12), our greatest reward will be eternal life in his presence.

11:19 In Old Testament days, the Ark of the Covenant was the most sacred treasure of the Israelite nation. For more information about the Ark, see the note on Exodus 37:1.

• **12:1–14:20** The seventh trumpet (11:15) ushers in the bowl judgments (15:1–16:21), but in the intervening chapters (12–14), John sees the conflict between God and Satan. He sees the source of all sin, evil, persecution, and suffering on the earth, and he understands why the great battle between the forces of God and Satan must soon take place. In these chapters the nature of evil is exposed, and Satan is seen in all his wickedness.

• **12:1-6** The woman represents God's faithful people who have been waiting for the Messiah; the crown of 12 stars represents the 12 tribes of Israel. God set apart the Jews for himself (Romans 9:4, 5), and that nation gave birth to the Messiah. The boy (Revelation 12:5) is Jesus, born to a devout Jewish girl named Mary (Luke 1:26-33). Evil King Herod immediately tried to destroy the infant Jesus (Matthew 2:13-20). Herod's desire to kill this newborn king, whom he saw as a threat to his throne, was motivated by Satan (the red dragon), who wanted to kill the world's Savior. The heavenly pageant of Revelation 12 shows that Christ's lowly birth in the town of Bethlehem had cosmic significance.

12:3, 4 The large red dragon, Satan, has seven heads, ten horns, and seven crowns, representing his power and the kingdoms of the world over which he rules. The stars that plunged to earth with him are usually considered to be the angels who fell with Satan and became his demons. According to Hebrew tradition, one-third of all the angels in heaven fell with Satan. For more on demons, see the notes on 9:3ff and Mark 5:1-20.

• **12:6** The wilderness represents a place of spiritual refuge and protection from Satan. Because God aided the woman's escape into the wilderness, we can be sure that he offers security to all true believers. Satan always attacks God's people, but God keeps them spiritually secure. Some will experience physical harm, but all will be protected from spiritual harm. God will not let Satan take the souls of God's true followers.

12:6 The 1,260 days (3½ years) is the same length of time that the dragon is allowed to exercise his authority (13:5) and that the holy city is trampled (see the second note on 11:3).

⁷Then there was war in heaven. Michael and the angels under his command fought the dragon and his angels. ⁸And the dragon lost the battle and was forced out of heaven. ⁹This great dragon—the ancient serpent called the Devil, or Satan, the one deceiving the whole world—was thrown down to the earth with all his angels.

¹⁰Then I heard a loud voice shouting across the heavens,

"It has happened at last—the salvation and power and kingdom of our God, and the authority of his Christ! For the Accuser has been thrown down to earth—the one who accused our brothers and sisters* before our God day and night. ¹¹And they have defeated him because of the blood of the Lamb and because of their testimony. And they were not afraid to die. ¹²Rejoice, O heavens! And you who live in the heavens, rejoice! But terror will come on the earth and the sea. For the Devil has come down to you in great anger, and he knows that he has little time."

¹³And when the dragon realized that he had been thrown down to the earth, he pursued the woman who had given birth to the child. ¹⁴But she was given two wings like those of a great eagle. This allowed her to fly to a place prepared for her in the wilderness, where she would be cared for and protected from the dragon* for a time, times, and half a time.

¹⁵Then the dragon tried to drown the woman with a flood of water that flowed from its mouth. ¹⁶But the earth helped her by opening its mouth and swallowing the river that gushed out from the mouth of the dragon. ¹⁷Then the dragon became angry at the woman, and he declared war against the rest of her children—all who keep God's commandments and confess that they belong to Jesus.

The Beast out of the Sea
¹⁸Then he stood* waiting on the shore of the sea.

12:10 Greek *brothers.*   **12:14** Greek *the serpent;* also in 12:15. See 12:9.   **12:18** Some manuscripts read *Then I stood,* and some translations put this entire sentence into 13:1.

Cross-references (margin):

12:7 Dan 10:13; 12:1 / Jude 1:9 / Rev 12:3

12:9 Gen 3:1 / Zech 3:1-2 / Matt 4:10 / Luke 10:18 / Rev 12:3; 20:2-10

12:10 Job 1:9-11 / Zech 3:1 / Rev 7:10; 11:15

12:11 Rev 2:10; 6:9; 7:14; 15:2

12:12 Rev 8:13; 18:20

12:14 Exod 19:4 / Dan 7:25; 12:7 / Rev 17:3, 18

12:17 Rev 1:2; 11:7; 13:7

12:7 This event fulfills Daniel 12:1ff. Michael is a high-ranking angel. One of his responsibilities is to guard God's community of believers.

12:7ff Much more happened at Christ's birth, death, and resurrection than most people realize. A war between the forces of good and evil was under way. With Christ's resurrection, Satan's ultimate defeat was assured. Some believe that Satan's fall to earth took place at Jesus' resurrection or ascension and that the 1,260 days (3½ years) is a symbolic way of referring to the time between Christ's first and second comings. Others say that Satan's defeat will occur in the middle of a literal seven-year tribulation period, following the rapture of the church and preceding the second coming of Christ and the beginning of Christ's 1,000-year reign. Whatever the case, we must remember that Christ is victorious—Satan has already been defeated because of Christ's death on the cross (12:10-12).

12:9 The Devil is not a symbol or legend; he is very real. Originally Satan was an angel of God, but through his own pride, he became corrupt. The Devil is God's enemy, and he constantly tries to hinder God's work, but he is limited by God's power and can do only what he is permitted to do (Job 1:6–2:8). The name *Satan* means "Accuser" (12:10). He actively looks for people to attack (1 Peter 5:8, 9). Satan likes to pursue believers who are vulnerable in their faith, who are spiritually weak, or who are isolated from other believers.

Even though God permits the Devil to do his work in this world, God is still in control. And Jesus has complete power over Satan—he defeated Satan when he died and rose again for the sins of everyone. One day Satan will be bound forever, never again to do his evil work (see 20:10).

12:10 Many believe that until this time, Satan still had access to God (see the note on Job 1:7ff). But here his access is forever barred (see also 9:1). He can no longer accuse people before God (see how Satan made accusations about Job before God in Job 1:6ff).

12:11 The critical blow to Satan came when the Lamb, Jesus Christ, shed his blood for our sins. The victory is won by sacrifice—Christ's death in our place to pay the penalty for our sin, and the sacrifices we make because of our faith in him. As we face the battle with Satan, we should not fear it or try to escape from it, but we should loyally serve Christ, who alone brings victory (see Romans 8:34-39).

• **12:12** The Devil begins to step up his persecution because he knows that "he has little time." We are living in the last days, and Satan's work has become more intense. Even though the Devil is very powerful, as we can see by the condition of our world, he is always under God's control. One of the reasons God allows Satan to work evil and bring temptation is so that those who pretend to be Christ's followers will be weeded out from Christ's true believers. Knowing that the last great confrontation with Jesus is near, Satan is desperately trying to recruit as great an enemy force as possible for this final battle.

12:17 While the woman (12:1) represents faithful Jews and the child (12:5) represents Christ, the rest of her children could be either Jewish believers or, most likely, all believers.

• **12:17** The apostle Paul tells us that we are in a spiritual battle (Ephesians 6:10-12). John says that the war is still being waged, but the outcome has already been determined. Satan and his followers have been defeated and will be destroyed. Nevertheless Satan is battling daily to bring more into his ranks and to keep his own from defecting to God's side. Those who belong to Christ have gone into battle on God's side, and he has guaranteed them victory. God will not lose the war, but we must make certain not to lose the battle for our own souls. Don't waver in your commitment to Christ. A great spiritual battle is being fought, and there is no time for indecision.

13:1
Dan 7:2-8
Rev 17:12

13:2
Dan 7:4-6
Rev 2:13; 12:3

13:3
2 Thes 2:9-12
Rev 17:8

13:5
Dan 7:8, 11, 20,
25; 11:36
2 Thes 2:4
Rev 11:2

13:7
Rev 5:9; 11:7

13:8
Dan 12:1

13:10
Jer 15:2; 43:11
Matt 26:52
Heb 6:12

13 And now in my vision I saw a beast rising up out of the sea. It had seven heads and ten horns, with ten crowns on its horns. And written on each head were names that blasphemed God. ²This beast looked like a leopard, but it had bear's feet and a lion's mouth! And the dragon gave him his own power and throne and great authority.

³I saw that one of the heads of the beast seemed wounded beyond recovery—but the fatal wound was healed! All the world marveled at this miracle and followed the beast in awe. ⁴They worshiped the dragon for giving the beast such power, and they worshiped the beast. "Is there anyone as great as the beast?" they exclaimed. "Who is able to fight against him?"

⁵Then the beast was allowed to speak great blasphemies against God. And he was given authority to do what he wanted for forty-two months. ⁶And he spoke terrible words of blasphemy against God, slandering his name and all who live in heaven, who are his temple. ⁷And the beast was allowed to wage war against God's holy people and to overcome them. And he was given authority to rule over every tribe and people and language and nation. ⁸And all the people who belong to this world worshiped the beast. They are the ones whose names were not written in the Book of Life, which belongs to the Lamb who was killed before the world was made.

⁹Anyone who is willing to hear should listen and understand. ¹⁰The people who are destined for prison will be arrested and taken away. Those who are destined for death

SATAN'S
WORK
IN THE
WORLD

His hatred for Christ 12:13
His hatred for God's people 12:17
His power and authority 13:2
His popularity among unbelievers 13:4
His blasphemy against God 13:6
His war against believers 13:7
His ability to deceive 13:14

13:1 This beast was initially identified with Rome because the Roman Empire, in its early days, encouraged an evil life-style, persecuted believers, and opposed God and his followers. But the beast also symbolizes the Antichrist—not Satan, but someone under Satan's power and control. This Antichrist looks like a combination of the four beasts that Daniel saw centuries earlier in a vision (Daniel 7). As the dragon (12:17) is in opposition to God, so the beast from the sea is against Christ and may be seen as Satan's false messiah. The early Roman Empire was strong and also anti-Christ (or against Christ's standards); many other individual powers throughout history have been anti-Christ. Many Christians believe that Satan's evil will culminate in a final Antichrist, one who will focus all the powers of evil against Jesus Christ and his followers.

• **13:1ff** Chapter 13 introduces Satan's (the dragon's) two evil accomplices: (1) the beast out of the sea (13:1ff) and (2) the beast out of the earth (13:11ff). Together, the three evil beings form an unholy trinity in direct opposition to the Holy Trinity of God the Father, God the Son, and God the Holy Spirit.

When Satan tempted Jesus in the wilderness, he wanted Jesus to show his power by turning stones into bread, to do miracles by jumping from a high place, and to gain political power by worshiping him (see Matthew 4:1-11). Satan's plan was to rule the world through Jesus, but Jesus refused to do Satan's bidding. Thus, Satan turns to the fearsome beasts described in Revelation. To the beast out of the sea he gives political power. To the beast out of the earth he gives power to do miracles. Both beasts work together to capture the control of the whole world. This unholy trinity—the dragon, the beast out of the sea, and the false prophet (see 16:13)—unite in a desperate attempt to overthrow God, but their efforts are doomed to failure. See what becomes of them in 19:19-21 and 20:10.

13:3ff Because the beast, the Antichrist, is a false messiah, he will be a counterfeit of Christ and will even stage a false resurrec-

tion (13:14). People will follow and worship him because they will be awed by his power and miracles (13:3, 4). He will unite the world under his leadership (13:7, 8), and he will control the world economy (13:16, 17). People are impressed by power and will follow those who display it forcefully or offer it to their followers. But those who follow the beast will only be fooling themselves: He will use his power to manipulate others, to point to himself, and to promote evil plans. God, by contrast, uses his infinitely greater power to love and to build up. Don't be misled by claims of great miracles or reports about a resurrection or reincarnation of someone claiming to be Christ. When Jesus returns, he will reveal himself to everyone (Matthew 24:23-28).

13:5 The power given to the beast will be limited by God. He will allow the beast to exercise authority only for a short time. Even while the beast is in power, God will still be in control (11:15; 12:10-12).

• **13:7** The beast will conquer God's people and rule over them, but he will not be able to harm them spiritually. He will establish worldwide dominance and demand that everyone worship him. And many *will* worship him—everyone except true believers. Refusal to worship the beast will result in temporary suffering for God's people, but they will be rewarded with eternal life in the end.

13:8 See the note on 3:5 for more information on the Book of Life.

13:10 In this time of persecution, being faithful to Christ could bring imprisonment and even execution. Some believers will be hurt or killed. But all that the beast and his followers will be able to do to believers is harm them physically; no spiritual harm will come to those whose faith in God is sincere. All believers will enter God's presence perfected and purified by the blood of the Lamb (7:9-17).

will be killed. But do not be dismayed, for here is your opportunity to have endurance and faith.

The Beast out of the Earth

[11] Then I saw another beast come up out of the earth. He had two horns like those of a lamb, and he spoke with the voice of a dragon. [12] He exercised all the authority of the first beast. And he required all the earth and those who belong to this world to worship the first beast, whose death-wound had been healed. [13] He did astounding miracles, such as making fire flash down to earth from heaven while everyone was watching. [14] And with all the miracles he was allowed to perform on behalf of the first beast, he deceived all the people who belong to this world. He ordered the people of the world to make a great statue of the first beast, who was fatally wounded and then came back to life. [15] He was permitted to give life to this statue so that it could speak. Then the statue commanded that anyone refusing to worship it must die.

[16] He required everyone—great and small, rich and poor, slave and free—to be given a mark on the right hand or on the forehead. [17] And no one could buy or sell anything without that mark, which was either the name of the beast or the number representing his name. [18] Wisdom is needed to understand this. Let the one who has understanding solve the number of the beast, for it is the number of a man.* His number is 666.*

The Lamb and the 144,000

14 Then I saw the Lamb standing on Mount Zion, and with him were 144,000 who had his name and his Father's name written on their foreheads. [2] And I heard a sound from heaven like the roaring of a great waterfall or the rolling of mighty thunder. It was like the sound of many harpists playing together.

[3] This great choir sang a wonderful new song in front of the throne of God and before the four living beings and the twenty-four elders. And no one could learn this song except

13:18a Or *of humanity.*   **13:18b** Some manuscripts read *616.*

13:11 Rev 13:1, 4
13:12 Rev 14:9; 19:20
13:13 1 Kgs 18:24-39 / Matt 24:24 / 2 Thes 2:9 / Rev 19:20
13:14 2 Thes 2:9 / Rev 12:9; 13:3, 12
13:15 Dan 3:3-6 / Rev 20:4
13:16 Rev 14:9; 19:18
13:17 Rev 14:9, 11; 16:2; 19:20; 20:4
13:18 Rev 17:9
14:1 Rev 3:12; 7:4
14:2 Rev 1:15; 19:6
14:3 Rev 4:4, 6

13:10 The times of great persecution that John saw will provide an opportunity for believers to exercise patient endurance and faithfulness. The tough times we face right now are also opportunities for spiritual growth. Don't fall into Satan's trap and turn away from God when hard times come. Instead, use those tough times as opportunities for growth.

13:11ff The first beast came out of the sea (13:1), but this second beast comes out of the earth. Later identified as the false prophet (16:13; 19:20), he is a counterfeit of the Holy Spirit. He seems to do good, but the purpose of his miracles is to deceive.

13:14 Throughout the Bible we see miracles performed as proofs of God's power, love, and authority. But here we see counterfeit miracles performed to deceive. This is a reminder of Pharaoh's magicians, who duplicated Moses' signs in Egypt. True signs and miracles point us to Jesus Christ, but miracles alone can be deceptive. That is why we must ask with respect to each miracle we see: Is this consistent with what God says in the Bible? The second beast here gains influence through the signs and wonders that he can perform on behalf of the first beast. The second beast orders the people to worship a statue in honor of the first beast—a direct flouting of the second commandment (Exodus 20:4-6). Allowing the Bible to guide our faith and practice will keep us from being deceived by false signs, however convincing they appear to be. Any teaching that contradicts God's Word is false.

13:16, 17 In every generation, Christians need to maintain a healthy skepticism about society's pleasures and rewards. In our educational, economic, and civic structures, there are incentives and rewards. Cooperating Christians must always support what is good and healthy about our society, but we must stand against sin. In some cases, such as Satan's system described here, the system or structure becomes so evil that there is no way to cooperate with it.

13:16-18 This mark of the beast is designed to mock the seal that God places on his followers (7:2, 3). Just as God marks his people to save them, so Satan's beast marks his people to save them from the persecution that Satan will inflict upon God's followers. Identifying this particular mark is not as important as identifying the purpose of the mark. Those who accept it show their allegiance to Satan, their willingness to operate within the economic system he promotes, and their rebellion against God. To refuse the mark means to commit oneself entirely to God, preferring death to compromising one's faith in Christ.

13:18 The meaning of this number has been discussed more than that of any other part of the book of Revelation. The three sixes have been said to represent many things, including the number of a man or the unholy trinity of Satan, the first beast, and the false prophet (16:13). If the number seven is considered to be the perfect number in the Bible, and if three sevens represent complete perfection, then the number 666 falls completely short of perfection. The first readers of this book probably applied the number to the emperor Nero, who symbolized all the evils of the Roman Empire. (The Greek letters of Nero's name represent numbers that total 666.) Whatever specific application the number is given, the number symbolizes the worldwide dominion and complete evil of this unholy trinity designed to undo Christ's work and overthrow him.

14:1ff Chapter 13 described the onslaught of evil that will occur when Satan and his helpers control the world. Chapter 14 gives a glimpse into eternity to show believers what awaits them if they endure. The Lamb is the Messiah. Mount Zion, often another name for Jerusalem, the capital of Israel, is contrasted with the worldly empire. The 144,000 represent believers who have endured persecutions on earth and now are ready to enjoy the eternal benefits and blessings of life with God forever. The three angels contrast the destiny of believers with that of unbelievers.

14:4
2 Cor 11:2

14:5
Isa 53:9
Zeph 3:13
1 Pet 2:22

14:6
Rev 5:9

14:7
Acts 4:24
Rev 15:4

14:8
Isa 21:9
Jer 51:8
Rev 16:19; 17:5;
18:2, 10

14:9
Rev 13:12-17

14:10
Ps 75:8
Isa 51:17, 22
Jer 25:15
Rev 16:19; 19:20;
20:10; 21:8

14:11
Isa 34:10
Rev 13:12-17

14:12
Rev 2:13; 12:17;
13:10

14:13
Heb 4:10

those 144,000 who had been redeemed from the earth. ⁴For they are spiritually unde-filed, pure as virgins,* following the Lamb wherever he goes. They have been purchased from among the people on the earth as a special offering* to God and to the Lamb. ⁵No falsehood can be charged against them; they are blameless.

The Three Angels

⁶And I saw another angel flying through the heavens, carrying the everlasting Good News to preach to the people who belong to this world—to every nation, tribe, language, and people. ⁷"Fear God," he shouted. "Give glory to him. For the time has come when he will sit as judge. Worship him who made heaven and earth, the sea, and all the springs of water."

⁸Then another angel followed him through the skies, shouting, "Babylon is fallen—that great city is fallen—because she seduced the nations of the world and made them drink the wine of her passionate immorality."

⁹Then a third angel followed them, shouting, "Anyone who worships the beast and his statue or who accepts his mark on the forehead or the hand ¹⁰must drink the wine of God's wrath. It is poured out undiluted into God's cup of wrath. And they will be tormented with fire and burning sulfur in the presence of the holy angels and the Lamb. ¹¹The smoke of their torment rises forever and ever, and they will have no relief day or night, for they have worshiped the beast and his statue and have accepted the mark of his name. ¹²Let this encourage God's holy people to endure persecution patiently and remain firm to the end, obeying his commands and trusting in Jesus."

¹³And I heard a voice from heaven saying, "Write this down: Blessed are those who die in the Lord from now on. Yes, says the Spirit, they are blessed indeed, for they will rest from all their toils and trials; for their good deeds follow them!"

14:4a Greek *they are virgins who have not defiled themselves with women.* **14:4b** Greek *as firstfruits.*

14:4 These people are true believers whose robes have been washed and made white in Christ's blood (7:14) through his death ("purchased from among the people on the earth"). In the Old Testament, idolatry was often portrayed as spiritual adultery (see the book of Hosea). Their purity is best understood symbolically, meaning that they are free from involvement with the pagan world system. These believers are spiritually pure: They have remained faithful to Christ, they have followed him exclusively, and they have received God's reward for staying committed to him. The "special offering" refers to the act of dedicating the first part (firstfruits) of the harvest as holy to God (Exodus 23:19; see also James 1:18).

• **14:6, 7** Some believe that this is a final, worldwide appeal to all people to recognize the one true God. No one will have the excuse of never hearing God's truth. Others, however, see this as an announcement of judgment rather than as an appeal. The people of the world have had their chance to proclaim their allegiance to God, and now God's great judgment is about to begin. If you are reading this, you have already heard God's truth. You know that God's final judgment will not be put off forever. Have you joyfully received the everlasting Good News? Have you confessed your sins and trusted in Christ to save you? If so, you have nothing to fear from God's judgment. The Judge of all the earth is your Savior!

14:8 Babylon was the name of both an evil city and an immoral empire, a world center for idol worship. Babylon ransacked Jerusalem and carried the people of Judah into captivity (see 2 Kings 25 and 2 Chronicles 36). Just as Babylon was the Jews' worst enemy, the Roman Empire was the worst enemy of the early Christians. John, who probably did not dare speak against Rome openly, applied the name *Babylon* to this enemy of God's people (Rome)—and, by extension, to all God's enemies of all times.

• **14:9-11** Those who worship the beast, accept his mark on their foreheads, and operate according to his world economic system will ultimately face God's judgment. Our world values money, power, and pleasure over God's leadership. To get what the world

values, many people deny God and violate Christian principles. Thus, they must drink of the wine of God's wrath (see Psalm 75; Isaiah 51:17).

14:11 The ultimate result of sin is unending separation from God. Because human beings are created in God's image with an inborn thirst for fellowship with him, separation from God will be the ultimate torment and misery. Sin always brings misery, but in this life we can choose to repent and restore our relationship with God. In eternity there will no longer be opportunity for repentance. If in this life we choose to be independent of God, in the next life we will be separated from him forever. Nobody is forced to choose eternal separation from God, and nobody suffers this fate by accident. Jesus invites all of us to open the door of our heart to him (3:20). If we do this, we will enjoy everlasting fellowship with him.

14:12 This news about God's ultimate triumph should encourage God's people to remain faithful through every trial and persecution. They can do this, God promises, by trusting in Jesus and obeying the commands found in his Word. The secret to enduring, therefore, is trust and obedience. Trust God to give you patience to endure even the small trials you face daily; obey him even when obedience is unattractive or dangerous.

• **14:13** While it is true that money, fame, and belongings can't be taken with us from this life, God's people *can* produce fruit that survives even death. God will remember our love, kindness, and faithfulness, and those who accept Christ through our witness will join us in the new earth. Be sure that your values are in line with God's values, and decide today to produce fruit that lasts forever.

The Harvest of the Earth

¹⁴Then I saw the Son of Man* sitting on a white cloud. He had a gold crown on his head and a sharp sickle in his hand.

14:14
Dan 7:13
Rev 1:13; 6:2

¹⁵Then an angel came from the Temple and called out in a loud voice to the one sitting on the cloud, "Use the sickle, for the time has come for you to harvest; the crop is ripe on the earth." ¹⁶So the one sitting on the cloud swung his sickle over the earth, and the whole earth was harvested.

14:15
Joel 3:13
Matt 13:39-40
Mark 4:29

¹⁷After that, another angel came from the Temple in heaven, and he also had a sharp sickle. ¹⁸Then another angel, who has power to destroy the world with fire, shouted to the angel with the sickle, "Use your sickle now to gather the clusters of grapes from the vines of the earth, for they are fully ripe for judgment." ¹⁹So the angel swung his sickle on the earth and loaded the grapes into the great winepress of God's wrath. ²⁰And the grapes were trodden in the winepress outside the city, and blood flowed from the winepress in a stream about 180 miles* long and as high as a horse's bridle.

14:18
Joel 3:13
Rev 6:9; 8:3; 14:15

14:19
Isa 63:2-3
Rev 19:15

14:20
Gen 49:11
Isa 63:3
Lam 1:15
Rev 19:15

5. Pouring out the seven plagues
The Song of Moses and of the Lamb

15 Then I saw in heaven another significant event, and it was great and marvelous. Seven angels were holding the seven last plagues, which would bring God's wrath to completion. ²I saw before me what seemed to be a crystal sea mixed with fire. And on it stood all the people who had been victorious over the beast and his statue and the number representing his name. They were all holding harps that God had given them. ³And they were singing the song of Moses, the servant of God, and the song of the Lamb:

15:1
Lev 26:21
Rev 15:6; 16:1;
21:9

15:2
Rev 4:6

15:3
Exod 15:1
Deut 32:4
Ps 145:17
Jer 10:7
Amos 3:13; 4:13
Rev 1:8; 4:8

"Great and marvelous are your actions,
   Lord God Almighty.
Just and true are your ways,
   O King of the nations.*
⁴ Who will not fear, O Lord, and glorify your name?
   For you alone are holy.
All nations will come and worship before you,
   for your righteous deeds have been revealed."

15:4
Ps 86:9
Jer 10:6-7
Mal 1:11

The Seven Bowls of the Seven Plagues

⁵Then I looked and saw that the Temple in heaven, God's Tabernacle, was thrown wide open! ⁶The seven angels who were holding the bowls of the seven plagues came from the Temple, clothed in spotless white linen* with gold belts across their chests. ⁷And one of the four living beings handed each of the seven angels a gold bowl filled with the terrible wrath of God, who lives forever and forever. ⁸The Temple was filled with smoke

15:5
Exod 38:21
Rev 11:19

15:6
Lev 26:21

15:8
Exod 40:34
1 Kgs 8:10-11
2 Chr 5:13-14
Isa 6:4

14:14 Or *one who looked like a man;* Greek reads *one like a son of man.*   **14:20** Greek *1,600 stadia* [296 kilometers]. **15:3** Some manuscripts read *King of the ages;* other manuscripts read *King of the saints.*   **15:6** Some manuscripts read *in bright and sparkling stone.*

• **14:14-16** This is an image of judgment: Christ is separating the faithful from the unfaithful like a farmer harvesting his crops. This is a time of joy for the Christians who have been persecuted and martyred—they will receive their long-awaited reward. Christians should not fear the Last Judgment. Jesus said, "I assure you, those who listen to my message and believe in God who sent me have eternal life. They will never be condemned for their sins, but they have already passed from death into life" (John 5:24).

14:19 A winepress was a large vat or trough where grapes were collected and then crushed. The juice flowed out of a duct that led into a large holding vat. The winepress is often used in the Bible as a symbol of God's wrath and judgment against sin (Isaiah 63:3-6; Lamentations 1:15; Joel 3:12, 13).

14:20 The distance of 180 miles is approximately the north-south length of Palestine.

• **15:1** The seven last plagues are also called the seven bowl judgments. They actually begin in chapter 16. Unlike the previous plagues, these are universal, and they will culminate in the abolition of all evil and the end of the world.

15:2 This is similar to the "sea of glass" described in 4:6, located before the throne of God. Here it is mixed with fire to represent wrath and judgment. Those who stand beside it are victorious over Satan and his evil beast.

15:3, 4 The song of Moses celebrated Israel's deliverance from Egypt (Exodus 15). The song of the Lamb celebrates the ultimate deliverance of God's people from the power of Satan.

• **15:5-8** This imagery brings us back to the time of the Exodus in the wilderness when the Ark of the Covenant (the symbol of God's presence among his people) resided in the Tabernacle. The angels coming out of the Temple are clothed in spotless white linen with gold belts across their chests. Their garments, reminiscent of the high priest's clothing, show that they are free from corruption, immorality, and injustice. The smoke that fills the Temple is the manifestation of God's glory and power. There is no escape from this judgment.

15:8 Our eternal reign with Christ won't begin until all evil is destroyed by his judgment. The faithful must wait for his timetable to be revealed.

from God's glory and power. No one could enter the Temple until the seven angels had completed pouring out the seven plagues.

16 Then I heard a mighty voice shouting from the Temple to the seven angels, "Now go your ways and empty out the seven bowls of God's wrath on the earth."

²So the first angel left the Temple and poured out his bowl over the earth, and horrible, malignant sores broke out on everyone who had the mark of the beast and who worshiped his statue.

³Then the second angel poured out his bowl on the sea, and it became like the blood of a corpse. And everything in the sea died.

⁴Then the third angel poured out his bowl on the rivers and springs, and they became blood. ⁵And I heard the angel who had authority over all water saying, "You are just in sending this judgment, O Holy One, who is and who always was. ⁶For your holy people and your prophets have been killed, and their blood was poured out on the earth. So you have given their murderers blood to drink. It is their just reward." ⁷And I heard a voice from the altar saying, "Yes, Lord God Almighty, your punishments are true and just."

⁸Then the fourth angel poured out his bowl on the sun, causing it to scorch everyone with its fire. ⁹Everyone was burned by this blast of heat, and they cursed the name of God, who sent all of these plagues. They did not repent and give him glory.

¹⁰Then the fifth angel poured out his bowl on the throne of the beast, and his kingdom was plunged into darkness. And his subjects ground their teeth in anguish, ¹¹and they cursed the God of heaven for their pains and sores. But they refused to repent of all their evil deeds.

¹²Then the sixth angel poured out his bowl on the great Euphrates River, and it dried up so that the kings from the east could march their armies westward without hindrance. ¹³And I saw three evil spirits that looked like frogs leap from the mouth of the dragon, the beast, and the false prophet. ¹⁴These miracle-working demons caused all the rulers of the world to gather for battle against the Lord on that great judgment day of God Almighty.

¹⁵"Take note: I will come as unexpectedly as a thief! Blessed are all who are watching for me, who keep their robes ready so they will not need to walk naked and ashamed."

¹⁶And they gathered all the rulers and their armies to a place called *Armageddon* in Hebrew.

16:1
Isa 66:6
Zeph 3:8
16:2
Exod 9:9-11
16:3
Exod 7:17-21
16:4
Exod 7:17-21
Ps 78:44
16:5
Rev 1:4, 8; 4:8;
11:17
16:6
Ps 79:3
Isa 49:26
16:7
Rev 1:8; 6:9;
14:18; 15:3; 19:2
16:10
Exod 10:21
Isa 8:22
Rev 8:12; 9:2; 13:2
16:11
Rev 9:20-21
16:12
Isa 11:15-16; 44:27
Jer 50:38; 51:36
16:13
Rev 12:3; 13:1,
11-17
16:14
Rev 6:17; 17:14;
19:19
16:15
1 Thes 5:2
Rev 3:3, 18
16:16
Judg 5:19
2 Kgs 9:27; 23:29
Zech 12:11

• **16:1ff** The bowl judgments are God's final and complete judgments on the earth. The end has come. There are many similarities between the bowl judgments and the trumpet judgments (8:6–11:19), but there are three main differences: (1) These judgments are complete whereas the trumpet judgments are partial; (2) the trumpet judgments still give unbelievers the opportunity to repent, but the bowl judgments do not; and (3) people are indirectly affected by several of the trumpet judgments but directly attacked by all the bowl judgments.

• **16:7** The significance of the altar itself responding is that *everyone and everything* will be praising God, acknowledging his righteousness and perfect justice.

• **16:9-21** We know that the people realize that these judgments come from God because they curse him for sending them. But they still refuse to recognize God's authority and repent of their sins. Christians should not be surprised at the hostility and hardness of heart of unbelievers. Even when the power of God is fully and completely revealed, many will still refuse to repent. If you find yourself ignoring God more and more, turn back to him now before your heart becomes too hard to repent (see the note on 9:20, 21 for more on hard hearts).

16:12 The Euphrates River was a natural protective boundary against the empires to the east (Babylon, Assyria, Persia). If it dried up, nothing could hold back invading armies. The armies from the east symbolize unhindered judgment.

16:13, 14 These evil spirits performing miraculous signs, who come out of the mouths of the unholy trinity, unite the rulers of the world for battle against God. The imagery of the demons coming out of the mouths of the three evil rulers signifies the verbal enticements and propaganda that will draw many people to their evil cause. For more about demons, see the note on 9:3ff.

• **16:15** Christ will return unexpectedly (1 Thessalonians 5:1-6), so we must be ready when he returns. We can prepare ourselves by standing firm in temptation and by being committed to God's moral standards. In what ways does your life show either your readiness or your lack of preparation for Christ's return?

• **16:16** This battlefield called Armageddon is near the city of Megiddo (southeast of the modern port of Haifa), which guarded a large plain in northern Israel. It is a strategic location near a prominent international highway leading north from Egypt through Israel, along the coast, and on to Babylon. Megiddo overlooked the entire plain southward toward Galilee and westward toward the mountains of Gilboa.

16:16 Sinful people will unite to fight against God in a final display of rebellion. Many are already united against Christ and his people—those who stand for truth, peace, justice, and morality. Your personal battle with evil foreshadows the great battle pictured here, where God will meet evil and destroy it once and for all. Be strong and courageous as you battle against sin and evil: You are fighting on the winning side.

[17]Then the seventh angel poured out his bowl into the air. And a mighty shout came from the throne of the Temple in heaven, saying, "It is finished!" [18]Then the thunder crashed and rolled, and lightning flashed. And there was an earthquake greater than ever before in human history. [19]The great city of Babylon split into three pieces, and cities around the world fell into heaps of rubble. And so God remembered all of Babylon's sins, and he made her drink the cup that was filled with the wine of his fierce wrath. [20]And every island disappeared, and all the mountains were leveled. [21]There was a terrible hailstorm, and hailstones weighing seventy-five pounds* fell from the sky onto the people below. They cursed God because of the hailstorm, which was a very terrible plague.

16:17
Isa 66:6
Rev 11:15; 21:6

16:18
Dan 12:1
Matt 24:21
Rev 4:5; 6:12

16:19
Rev 14:8, 10

16:20
Rev 6:14; 20:11

16:21
Exod 9:23-25
Rev 11:19; 16:9, 11

6. Seizing the final victory
The Great Prostitute

17 One of the seven angels who had poured out the seven bowls came over and spoke to me. "Come with me," he said, "and I will show you the judgment that is going to come on the great prostitute, who sits on many waters. [2]The rulers of the world have had immoral relations with her, and the people who belong to this world have been made drunk by the wine of her immorality."

17:1
Jer 51:13
Rev 17:15; 19:2

17:2
Jer 51:7
Rev 14:8; 18:3

[3]So the angel took me in spirit* into the wilderness. There I saw a woman sitting on a scarlet beast that had seven heads and ten horns, written all over with blasphemies against God. [4]The woman wore purple and scarlet clothing and beautiful jewelry made of gold and precious gems and pearls. She held in her hand a gold goblet full of obscenities and the impurities of her immorality. [5]A mysterious name was written on her forehead: "Babylon the Great, Mother of All Prostitutes and Obscenities in the World." [6]I could see that she was drunk—drunk with the blood of God's holy people who were witnesses for Jesus. I stared at her completely amazed.

17:3
Rev 1:10; 12:6;
13:1

17:4
Jer 51:7
Ezek 28:13

17:5
2 Thes 2:7
Rev 17:2, 7

17:6
Rev 16:6; 18:24

[7]"Why are you so amazed?" the angel asked. "I will tell you the mystery of this woman and of the beast with seven heads and ten horns. [8]The beast you saw was alive but isn't now. And yet he will soon come up out of the bottomless pit and go to eternal destruction. And the people who belong to this world, whose names were not written in the Book of Life from before the world began, will be amazed at the reappearance of this beast who had died.

17:8
Dan 12:1
Rev 11:7; 13:1, 3

[9]"And now understand this: The seven heads of the beast represent the seven hills of the city where this woman rules. They also represent seven kings. [10]Five kings have already fallen, the sixth now reigns, and the seventh is yet to come, but his reign will be brief. [11]The scarlet beast that was alive and then died is the eighth king. He is like the

17:9
Rev 13:18

16:21 Greek *1 talent* [34 kilograms].   **17:3** Or *in the Spirit.*

16:17-21 For more information on Babylon and what it represents in Revelation, see the note on 14:8. The city's division into three sections is a symbol of its complete destruction.

• **17:1ff** The destruction of Babylon mentioned in 16:17-21 is now described in greater detail. The "great prostitute," called Babylon, represents the early Roman Empire with its many gods and the blood of Christian martyrs on its hands. The water stands for either sea commerce or a well-watered (well-provisioned) city. The great prostitute represents the seductiveness of the governmental system that uses immoral means to gain its own pleasure, prosperity, and advantage. In contrast to the prostitute, Christ's bride, the church, is pure and obedient (19:6-9). The wicked city of Babylon contrasts with the heavenly city of Jerusalem (21:10–22:5). The original readers probably rather quickly identified Babylon with Rome, but Babylon also symbolizes any system that is hostile to God (see 17:5).

17:3 The scarlet beast is either the dragon of 12:3 or the beast out of the sea described in 13:1.

• **17:6** Throughout history, people have been killed for their faith. Over the last century, millions have been killed by oppressive governments, and many of those victims were believers. The woman's drunkenness shows her pleasure in her evil accomplishments and her false feeling of triumph over the church. But every martyr who has fallen before her sword has only served to strengthen the faith of the church.

17:8 In chapter 12 we met the dragon (Satan). In chapter 13 we saw the beast from the sea and the power he received from Satan. In chapters 14–16 we see God's great judgments. In this chapter, a scarlet beast similar to the beast and the dragon appears as an ally of the great prostitute. The beast was alive, died, and then came back to life. The beast's resurrection symbolizes the persistence of evil. This resurgence of evil power will convince many to join forces with the beast, but those who choose the side of evil condemn themselves to the Devil's fate—eternal torment.

17:8 For more information on the Book of Life, see the note on 3:5.

17:9-11 Here John is referring to Rome, the city famous for its seven hills. Many say that this city also symbolized all evil in the world—any person, religion, group, government, or structure that opposed Christ. Whatever view is taken of the seven hills and seven kings, this section indicates the climax of Satan's struggle against God. Evil's power is limited, and its destruction is on the horizon.

17:12
Dan 7:20, 24
Rev 18:10, 17, 19

17:14
Matt 22:14
1 Tim 6:15

17:15
Isa 8:7
Jer 47:2
Rev 13:7; 17:1

17:16
Lev 21:9
Ezek 16:37, 39
Rev 18:8, 19

17:17
Rev 10:7; 17:13

17:18
Rev 16:19

other seven, and he, too, will go to his doom. ¹²His ten horns are ten kings who have not yet risen to power; they will be appointed to their kingdoms for one brief moment to reign with the beast. ¹³They will all agree to give their power and authority to him. ¹⁴Together they will wage war against the Lamb, but the Lamb will defeat them because he is Lord over all lords and King over all kings, and his people are the called and chosen and faithful ones."

¹⁵And the angel said to me, "The waters where the prostitute is sitting represent masses of people of every nation and language. ¹⁶The scarlet beast and his ten horns—which represent ten kings who will reign with him—all hate the prostitute. They will strip her naked, eat her flesh, and burn her remains with fire. ¹⁷For God has put a plan into their minds, a plan that will carry out his purposes. They will mutually agree to give their authority to the scarlet beast, and so the words of God will be fulfilled. ¹⁸And this woman you saw in your vision represents the great city that rules over the kings of the earth."

The Fall of Babylon

18:2
Isa 13:19-22; 21:9
Jer 50:39

18:3
Ezek 27:9-25

18:4
Isa 48:20; 52:11
Jer 51:6, 9, 45

18:5
Jer 51:9

18:6
Jer 50:15, 29

18:7
Isa 47:8

18:8
Isa 47:9
Jer 50:31-34

18 After all this I saw another angel come down from heaven with great authority, and the earth grew bright with his splendor. ²He gave a mighty shout, "Babylon is fallen—that great city is fallen! She has become the hideout of demons and evil spirits, a nest for filthy buzzards, and a den for dreadful beasts. ³For all the nations have drunk the wine of her passionate immorality. The rulers of the world have committed adultery with her, and merchants throughout the world have grown rich as a result of her luxurious living."

⁴Then I heard another voice calling from heaven, "Come away from her, my people. Do not take part in her sins, or you will be punished with her. ⁵For her sins are piled as high as heaven, and God is ready to judge her for her evil deeds. ⁶Do to her as she has done to your people. Give her a double penalty for all her evil deeds. She brewed a cup of terror for others, so give her twice as much as she gave out. ⁷She has lived in luxury and pleasure, so match it now with torments and sorrows. She boasts, 'I am queen on my throne. I am no helpless widow. I will not experience sorrow.' ⁸Therefore, the sorrows

---

HOW CAN A PERSON KEEP AWAY FROM THE EVIL SYSTEM?
Here are some suggestions:

1. People must always be more important than products.
2. Keep away from pride in your own programs, plans, and successes.
3. Remember that God's will and Word must never be compromised.
4. People must always be considered above the making of money.
5. Do what is right, no matter what the cost.
6. Be involved in businesses that provide worthwhile products or services—not just things that feed the world's desires.

● **17:12** The 10 horns represent kings of nations yet to arise. Rome will be followed by other powers. Rome is a good example of how the Antichrist's system will work, demanding complete allegiance and ruling by raw power, oppression, and slavery. Whoever the 10 kings are, they will give their power to the Antichrist and make war against the Lamb.

● **17:16** In a dramatic turn of events, the prostitute's allies turn on her and destroy her. This is how evil operates. Destructive by its very nature, it discards its own adherents when they cease to serve its purposes. An unholy alliance is an uneasy alliance because each partner puts its own interests first.

● **17:17** No matter what happens, we must trust that God is still in charge, that God overrules all the plans and intrigues of the evil one, and that God's plans will happen just as he says. God even uses people opposed to him as tools to execute his will. Although he allows evil to permeate this present world, the new earth will never know sin.

● **18:1ff** This chapter shows the complete destruction of Babylon, John's metaphorical name for the evil world power and all it represents. Everything that tries to block God's purposes will come to a violent end. For more information on how the book of Revelation uses the name *Babylon*, see the note on 14:8.

● **18:2, 3** Merchants in the Roman Empire grew rich by exploiting the sinful pleasures of their society. Many businesspeople today do the same thing. Businesses and governments are often based on greed, money, and power. Many bright individuals are tempted to take advantage of an evil system to enrich themselves. Christians are warned to stay free from the lure of money, status, and the good life. We are to live according to the values Christ exemplified: service, giving, self-sacrifice, obedience, and truth.

● **18:4-8** The people of Babylon had lived in luxury and pleasure. The city boasted, "I am queen on my throne. . . . I will not experience sorrow." The powerful, wealthy people of this world are susceptible to this same attitude. A person who is financially comfortable often feels invulnerable, secure, and in control, feeling no need for God or anyone else. This kind of attitude defies God, and his judgment against it is harsh. We are told to avoid Babylon's sins. If you are financially secure, don't become complacent and deluded by the myth of self-sufficiency. Use your resources to help others and advance God's Kingdom.

of death and mourning and famine will overtake her in a single day. She will be utterly consumed by fire, for the Lord God who judges her is mighty."

⁹And the rulers of the world who took part in her immoral acts and enjoyed her great luxury will mourn for her as they see the smoke rising from her charred remains. ¹⁰They will stand at a distance, terrified by her great torment. They will cry out, "How terrible, how terrible for Babylon, that great city! In one single moment God's judgment came on her."

¹¹The merchants of the world will weep and mourn for her, for there is no one left to buy their goods. ¹²She bought great quantities of gold, silver, jewels, pearls, fine linen, purple dye, silk, scarlet cloth, every kind of perfumed wood, ivory goods, objects made of expensive wood, bronze, iron, and marble. ¹³She also bought cinnamon, spice, incense, myrrh, frankincense, wine, olive oil, fine flour, wheat, cattle, sheep, horses, chariots, and slaves—yes, she even traded in human lives.

¹⁴"All the fancy things you loved so much are gone," they cry. "The luxuries and splendor that you prized so much will never be yours again. They are gone forever."

¹⁵The merchants who became wealthy by selling her these things will stand at a distance, terrified by her great torment. They will weep and cry. ¹⁶"How terrible, how terrible for that great city! She was so beautiful—like a woman clothed in finest purple and scarlet linens, decked out with gold and precious stones and pearls! ¹⁷And in one single moment all the wealth of the city is gone!"

And all the shipowners and captains of the merchant ships and their crews will stand at a distance. ¹⁸They will weep as they watch the smoke ascend, and they will say, "Where in all the world is there another city like this?" ¹⁹And they will throw dust on their heads to show their great sorrow. And they will say, "How terrible, how terrible for the great city! She made us all rich from her great wealth. And now in a single hour it is all gone."

²⁰But you, O heaven, rejoice over her fate. And you also rejoice, O holy people of God and apostles and prophets! For at last God has judged her on your behalf.

²¹Then a mighty angel picked up a boulder as large as a great millstone. He threw it into the ocean and shouted, "Babylon, the great city, will be thrown down as violently as I have thrown away this stone, and she will disappear forever. ²²Never again will the sound of music be heard there—no more harps, songs, flutes, or trumpets. There will be no industry of any kind, and no more milling of grain. ²³Her nights will be dark, without a single lamp. There will be no happy voices of brides and grooms. This will happen because her merchants, who were the greatest in the world, deceived the nations with her sorceries. ²⁴In her streets the blood of the prophets was spilled. She was the one who slaughtered God's people all over the world."

Songs of Victory in Heaven

19 After this, I heard the sound of a vast crowd in heaven shouting, "Hallelujah! Salvation is from our God. Glory and power belong to him alone. ²His judgments are just and true. He has punished the great prostitute who corrupted the earth with her

18:9
Ps 58:10
Ezek 26:16
Rev 17:2

18:10
Ezek 26:17
Rev 14:8

18:11
Ezek 27:27, 36
Rev 18:3

18:12-13
Ezek 27:12-22

18:15
Ezek 27:36

18:16
Rev 17:4

18:17
Ezek 27:27-29
Rev 17:16

18:18
Ezek 27:32
Rev 13:4

18:19
Ezek 27:30-34

18:20
Jer 51:48
Rev 12:12; 19:2

18:21
Jer 51:63

18:22
Ezek 26:13

18:23
Jer 7:34; 16:9;
25:10
Nah 3:4

18:24
Jer 51:49
Matt 23:35-37
Rev 16:6; 17:6

19:1
Rev 4:11; 7:10;
12:10

• **18:9, 10** Those who are tied to the world's system will lose everything when it collapses. What they have worked for a lifetime to build up will be destroyed in one hour. Those who work only for material rewards will have nothing when they die or when their possessions are destroyed. What can we take with us to the new earth? Our faith, our Christian character, and our relationships with other believers. These are more important than any amount of money, power, or pleasure.

18:9-19 Those who are in control of various parts of the economic system will mourn at Babylon's fall. The political leaders will mourn because they were the overseers of Babylon's wealth and were in a position to enrich themselves greatly. The merchants will mourn because Babylon, the greatest customer for their goods, will be gone. The sea captains will no longer have anywhere to bring their goods because the merchants will have nowhere to sell them. The fall of the evil world system affects all who enjoyed and depended on it. No one will remain unaffected by Babylon's fall.

• **18:11-13** This list of various merchandise illustrates the extreme materialism of this society. Few of these goods are necessities—

most are luxuries. The society had become so self-indulgent that people were willing to use evil means to gratify their desires. Even people had become commodities—people were sold as slaves to Babylon.

18:11-19 God's people should not live for money, because money will be worthless in eternity. And they should keep on guard constantly against greed, a sin that is always ready to take over their lives.

• **19:1ff** Praise is the heartfelt response to God by those who love him. The more you get to know God and realize what he has done, the more you will respond with praise. Praise is at the heart of true worship. Let your praise of God flow out of your realization of who he is and how much he loves you.

19:1, 2 The identity of this great prostitute is explained in the note on 17:1ff.

• **19:1-8** A vast crowd in heaven initiates the chorus of praise to God for his victory (19:1-3). Then the 24 elders (identified in the note on 4:4) join the chorus (19:4). Finally, the great choir of heaven once again praises God—the wedding of the Lamb

19:3
Isa 34:10
Rev 14:11

19:4
Rev 4:4, 6, 10

19:5
Pss 115:13; 134:1;
135:1
Rev 11:18

19:6
Rev 11:15

19:7
Matt 22:2; 25:10
Eph 5:32
Rev 21:2, 9

19:9
Luke 14:15
Rev 21:5; 22:6

19:10
Acts 10:25-26
Rev 22:8-9

19:11
Isa 11:4
Rev 1:14; 3:14

19:12
Rev 2:17

19:13
Isa 63:1-3
John 1:1, 14
1 Jn 1:1-2

19:14
Rev 3:4

19:15
Isa 11:4; 63:3
2 Thes 2:8
Rev 2:27; 14:20

19:16
Rev 17:14

19:17-18
Ezek 39:17-20

immorality, and he has avenged the murder of his servants." ³Again and again their voices rang, "Hallelujah! The smoke from that city ascends forever and forever!"

⁴Then the twenty-four elders and the four living beings fell down and worshiped God, who was sitting on the throne. They cried out, "Amen! Hallelujah!"

⁵And from the throne came a voice that said, "Praise our God, all his servants, from the least to the greatest, all who fear him."

⁶Then I heard again what sounded like the shout of a huge crowd, or the roar of mighty ocean waves, or the crash of loud thunder: "Hallelujah! For the Lord our God, the Almighty, reigns. ⁷Let us be glad and rejoice and honor him. For the time has come for the wedding feast of the Lamb, and his bride has prepared herself. ⁸She is permitted to wear the finest white linen." (Fine linen represents the good deeds done by the people of God.)

⁹And the angel said, "Write this: Blessed are those who are invited to the wedding feast of the Lamb." And he added, "These are true words that come from God."

¹⁰Then I fell down at his feet to worship him, but he said, "No, don't worship me. For I am a servant of God, just like you and other brothers and sisters* who testify of their faith in Jesus. Worship God. For the essence of prophecy is to give a clear witness for Jesus.*"

The Rider on the White Horse

¹¹Then I saw heaven opened, and a white horse was standing there. And the one sitting on the horse was named Faithful and True. For he judges fairly and then goes to war. ¹²His eyes were bright like flames of fire, and on his head were many crowns. A name was written on him, and only he knew what it meant. ¹³He was clothed with a robe dipped in blood, and his title was the Word of God. ¹⁴The armies of heaven, dressed in pure white linen, followed him on white horses. ¹⁵From his mouth came a sharp sword, and with it he struck down the nations. He ruled them with an iron rod, and he trod the winepress of the fierce wrath of almighty God. ¹⁶On his robe and thigh was written this title: King of kings and Lord of lords.

¹⁷Then I saw an angel standing in the sun, shouting to the vultures flying high in the sky: "Come! Gather together for the great banquet God has prepared. ¹⁸Come and eat the flesh of kings, captains, and strong warriors; of horses and their riders; and of all humanity, both free and slave, small and great."

¹⁹Then I saw the beast gathering the kings of the earth and their armies in order to fight

19:10a Greek *brothers.*   **19:10b** Or *is the message confirmed by Jesus.*

---

has come (19:6-8). See Matthew 25:1-13 where Christ compares the coming of his Kingdom to a wedding for which we must be prepared.

19:7, 8 This is the culmination of human history—the judgment of the wicked and the wedding of the Lamb and his bride, the church. The church consists of all faithful believers from all time. The bride's clothing stands in sharp contrast to the gaudy clothing of the great prostitute of 17:4 and 18:16. The bride's clothing represents the good deeds of the believers. These good deeds are not done by believers to their merit, but they reflect the work of Christ to save us (7:9, 14).

• **19:10** The angel did not accept John's homage and worship because only God is worthy of worship. Like John, it would be easy for us to become overwhelmed by this prophetic pageant. But Jesus is the central focus of God's revelation and his redemptive plan (as announced by the prophets). As you read the book of Revelation, don't get bogged down in all the details of the awesome visions; remember that the overarching theme in all the visions is the ultimate victory of Jesus Christ over evil.

19:11 The name "Faithful and True" contrasts with the faithless and deceitful Babylon described in chapter 18.

• **19:11-21** John's vision shifts again. Heaven opens, and Jesus appears—this time not as a Lamb but as a warrior on a white horse (symbolizing victory). Jesus came first as a Lamb to be a sacrifice for sin, but he will return as a conqueror and king to execute judgment (2 Thessalonians 1:7-10). Jesus' first coming brought forgiveness; his second will bring judgment. The battle lines have been drawn between God and evil, and the world is waiting for the King to ride onto the field.

19:12 Although Jesus is called "Faithful and True" (19:11), "Word of God" (19:13), and "King of kings and Lord of lords" (19:16), this verse implies that no name can do him justice. He is greater than any description or expression the human mind can devise.

19:13 For more about the symbolism of Jesus' clothes being dipped in blood, see the second note on 7:14.

19:16 This title indicates our God's sovereignty. Most of the world is worshiping the beast, the Antichrist, whom they believe has all power and authority. Then suddenly out of heaven ride Christ and his army of angels—the "King of kings and Lord of lords." His entrance signals the end of the false powers.

19:17 This "great banquet" is a grim contrast to the wedding feast of the Lamb (19:9). One is a celebration; the other is devastation.

19:19 The beast is identified in the note on 13:1.

19:19-21 The battle lines have been drawn, and the greatest confrontation in the history of the world is about to begin. The beast (the Antichrist) and the false prophet have gathered the governments and armies of the earth under the Antichrist's rule. The enemy armies believe they have come of their own volition; in reality, God has summoned them to battle in order to defeat them. That they would even presume to fight against God shows how their pride and rebellion have distorted their thinking. There really is no fight, however, because the victory was won when Jesus died on the cross for sin and rose from the dead. Thus, the evil leaders are immediately captured and sent to their punishment, and the forces of evil are annihilated.

against the one sitting on the horse and his army. ²⁰And the beast was captured, and with him the false prophet who did mighty miracles on behalf of the beast—miracles that deceived all who had accepted the mark of the beast and who worshiped his statue. Both the beast and his false prophet were thrown alive into the lake of fire that burns with sulfur. ²¹Their entire army was killed by the sharp sword that came out of the mouth of the one riding the white horse. And all the vultures of the sky gorged themselves on the dead bodies.

19:20
Isa 30:33
Dan 7:11
Rev 13:12-16;
20:10, 14-15; 21:8

The Thousand Years

20 Then I saw an angel come down from heaven with the key to the bottomless pit and a heavy chain in his hand. ²He seized the dragon—that old serpent, the Devil, Satan—and bound him in chains for a thousand years. ³The angel threw him into the bottomless pit, which he then shut and locked so Satan could not deceive the nations anymore until the thousand years were finished. Afterward he would be released again for a little while.

20:1
Rev 1:18; 10:1

20:2
Rev 12:9

20:3
2 Pet 2:4
Jude 1:6

⁴Then I saw thrones, and the people sitting on them had been given the authority to judge. And I saw the souls of those who had been beheaded for their testimony about Jesus, for proclaiming the word of God. And I saw the souls of those who had not worshiped the beast or his statue, nor accepted his mark on their forehead or their hands. They came to life again, and they reigned with Christ for a thousand years. ⁵This is the first resurrection. (The rest of the dead did not come back to life until the thousand years had ended.) ⁶Blessed and holy are those who share in the first resurrection. For them the second death holds no power, but they will be priests of God and of Christ and will reign with him a thousand years.

20:4
Dan 7:9, 22, 27
Matt 19:28
Rev 13:12-16

20:5
Ezek 37:10
Luke 14:14

20:6
1 Pet 2:5, 9
Rev 1:6; 5:10;
20:14

The Defeat of Satan

⁷When the thousand years end, Satan will be let out of his prison. ⁸He will go out to deceive the nations from every corner of the earth, which are called Gog and Magog. He will gather them together for battle—a mighty host, as numberless as sand along the

20:7
Rev 20:2

20:8
Ezek 7:2; 38:2

19:20 The lake of fire that burns with sulfur is the final destination of the wicked. This lake is different from the bottomless pit referred to in 9:1. The Antichrist and the false prophet are thrown into the lake of fire. Then their leader, Satan himself, will be thrown into that lake (20:10), and finally death and the grave (20:14). Afterward, everyone whose name is not recorded in the Book of Life will be thrown into the lake of fire (20:15).

20:1 The angel and the bottomless pit are explained in the notes on 9:1 and 19:20.

20:2 The dragon, Satan, is discussed in more detail in the notes on 12:3, 4 and 12:9. The dragon is not bound as punishment—that occurs in 20:10—but so that he cannot deceive the nations.

• **20:2-4** The 1,000 years are often referred to as the *Millennium* (Latin for 1,000). Just how and when this 1,000 years takes place is understood differently among Christian scholars. The three major positions on this issue are called postmillennialism, premillennialism, and amillennialism.

(1) *Postmillennialism* looks for a literal 1,000-year period of peace on earth ushered in by the church. At the end of the 1,000 years, Satan will be unleashed once more, but then Christ will return to defeat him and reign forever. Christ's second coming will not occur until after the 1,000-year period.

(2) *Premillennialism* also views the 1,000 years as a literal time period but holds that Christ's second coming initiates his 1,000-year reign and that this reign occurs before the final removal of Satan.

(3) *Amillennialism* understands the 1,000-year period to be symbolic of the time between Christ's ascension and his return. This Millennium is the reign of Christ in the hearts of believers and in his church; thus, it is another way of referring to the church age. This period will end with the second coming of Christ.

These different views about the Millennium need not cause division and controversy in the church because each view acknowledges what is most crucial to Christianity: Christ will return, defeat Satan, and reign forever! Whatever and whenever the Millennium is, Jesus Christ will unite all believers; therefore, we should not let this issue divide us.

• **20:3** John doesn't say why God once again sets Satan free, but it is part of God's plan for judging the world. Perhaps it is to expose those who rebel against God in their hearts and confirm those who are truly faithful to God. Whatever the reason, Satan's release results in the final destruction of all evil (20:12-15).

20:4 The beast's mark is explained in the note on 13:16-18.

• **20:5, 6** Christians hold two basic views concerning this first resurrection: (1) Some believe that the first resurrection is spiritual (in our heart at salvation) and that the Millennium is our spiritual reign with Christ between his first and second comings. During this time, we are priests of God because Christ reigns in our hearts. In this view, the second resurrection is the bodily resurrection of all people for judgment. (2) Others believe that the first resurrection occurs after Satan has been set aside. It is a physical resurrection of believers, who then reign with Christ on the earth for a literal 1,000 years. The second resurrection occurs at the end of this Millennium in order to judge unbelievers who have died.

• **20:6** The second death is spiritual death—everlasting separation from God (see 21:8).

20:7-9 Gog and Magog symbolize all the forces of evil that band together to battle God. Noah's son Japheth had a son named Magog (Genesis 10:2). Ezekiel presents Gog as a leader of forces against Israel (Ezekiel 38–39).

20:9
Ps 87:2
Ezek 38:22; 39:6

shore. ⁹And I saw them as they went up on the broad plain of the earth and surrounded God's people and the beloved city. But fire from heaven came down on the attacking armies and consumed them.

20:10
Rev 14:10; 19:20;
20:15

¹⁰Then the Devil, who betrayed them, was thrown into the lake of fire that burns with sulfur, joining the beast and the false prophet. There they will be tormented day and night forever and ever.

The Final Judgment

20:11-12
Dan 7:9-10
Matt 25:31-46

20:13
Isa 26:19
Matt 16:27
John 5:28
Rev 1:18

20:14
1 Cor 15:26, 55
Rev 19:20

¹¹And I saw a great white throne, and I saw the one who was sitting on it. The earth and sky fled from his presence, but they found no place to hide. ¹²I saw the dead, both great and small, standing before God's throne. And the books were opened, including the Book of Life. And the dead were judged according to the things written in the books, according to what they had done. ¹³The sea gave up the dead in it, and death and the grave* gave up the dead in them. They were all judged according to their deeds. ¹⁴And death and the grave were thrown into the lake of fire. This is the second death—the lake of fire. ¹⁵And anyone whose name was not found recorded in the Book of Life was thrown into the lake of fire.

7. Making all things new

The New Jerusalem

21:1
Isa 65:17; 66:22

21:2
Isa 52:1; 61:10

21 Then I saw a new heaven and a new earth, for the old heaven and the old earth had disappeared. And the sea was also gone. ²And I saw the holy city, the new Jerusalem, coming down from God out of heaven like a beautiful bride prepared for her husband.

20:13 Greek *and Hades;* also in 20:14.

THE BEGINNING AND THE END

Genesis	Revelation
The sun is created.	The sun is not needed.
Satan is victorious.	Satan is defeated.
Sin enters the human race.	Sin is banished.
People run and hide from God.	People are invited to live with God forever.
People are cursed.	The curse is removed.
Tears are shed, with sorrow for sin.	No more sin, no more tears or sorrow.
The garden and earth are cursed.	God's city is glorified; the earth is made new.
Paradise is lost.	Paradise is regained.
People are doomed to death.	Death is defeated; believers live forever with God.

The Bible records for us the beginning of the world and the end of the world. The story of mankind, from beginning to end—from the fall into sin to redemption and God's ultimate victory over evil—is found in the pages of the Bible.

• **20:9** This is not a typical battle where the outcome is in doubt during the heat of the conflict. Here there is no contest. Two mighty forces of evil—those of the beast (19:19) and of Satan (20:8)—unite to do battle against God. The Bible uses just two verses to describe each battle: The evil beast and his forces are captured and thrown into the lake of fire (19:20, 21), and fire from heaven devours Satan and his attacking armies (20:9, 10). For God, it is as easy as that. There will be no doubt, no worry, no second thoughts for believers about whether they have chosen the right side. If you are with God, you will experience this tremendous victory with Christ.

• **20:10** Satan's power is not eternal—he will meet his doom. He began his evil work in people at the beginning (Genesis 3:1-6) and continues it today, but he will be destroyed when he is thrown into the lake of fire. The Devil will be released from the bottomless pit ("his prison," 20:7), but he will never be released from the lake of fire. He will never be a threat to anyone again.

20:12-15 At the judgment, the books are opened. They represent God's judgment, and in them are recorded the deeds of everyone, good or evil. We are not saved by deeds, but deeds are seen as clear evidence of a person's actual relationship with

God. The Book of Life contains the names of those who have put their trust in Christ to save them.

• **20:14** Death and the grave are thrown into the lake of fire. God's judgment is finished. The lake of fire is the ultimate destination of everything wicked—Satan, the beast, the false prophet, the demons, death, the grave, and all those whose names are not recorded in the Book of Life because they did not place their faith in Jesus Christ. John's vision does not permit any gray areas in God's judgment. If by faith we have not identified with Christ, confessing him as Lord, there will be no hope, no second chance, no other appeal.

• **21:1** The earth as we know it will not last forever, but after God's great judgment, he will create a new earth (see Romans 8:18-21; 2 Peter 3:7-13). God had also promised Isaiah that he would create a new and eternal earth (Isaiah 65:17; 66:22). The sea in John's time was viewed as dangerous and changeable. It was also the source of the beast (13:1). We don't know how the new earth will look or where it will be, but God and his followers—those whose names are written in the Book of Life—will be united to live there forever. Will you be there?

• **21:2, 3** The new Jerusalem is where God lives among his people. Instead of our going up to meet him, he comes down

³I heard a loud shout from the throne, saying, "Look, the home of God is now among his people! He will live with them, and they will be his people. God himself will be with them.* ⁴He will remove all of their sorrows, and there will be no more death or sorrow or crying or pain. For the old world and its evils are gone forever."

⁵And the one sitting on the throne said, "Look, I am making all things new!" And then he said to me, "Write this down, for what I tell you is trustworthy and true." ⁶And he also said, "It is finished! I am the Alpha and the Omega—the Beginning and the End. To all who are thirsty I will give the springs of the water of life without charge! ⁷All who are victorious will inherit all these blessings, and I will be their God, and they will be my children. ⁸But cowards who turn away from me, and unbelievers, and the corrupt, and murderers, and the immoral, and those who practice witchcraft, and idol worshipers, and all liars—their doom is in the lake that burns with fire and sulfur. This is the second death."

⁹Then one of the seven angels who held the seven bowls containing the seven last plagues came and said to me, "Come with me! I will show you the bride, the wife of the Lamb."

¹⁰So he took me in spirit* to a great, high mountain, and he showed me the holy city, Jerusalem, descending out of heaven from God. ¹¹It was filled with the glory of God and sparkled like a precious gem, crystal clear like jasper. ¹²Its walls were broad and high, with twelve gates guarded by twelve angels. And the names of the twelve tribes of Israel were written on the gates. ¹³There were three gates on each side—east, north, south, and west. ¹⁴The wall of the city had twelve foundation stones, and on them were written the names of the twelve apostles of the Lamb.

¹⁵The angel who talked to me held in his hand a gold measuring stick to measure the city, its gates, and its wall. ¹⁶When he measured it, he found it was a square, as wide as it was long. In fact, it was in the form of a cube, for its length and width and height were each 1,400 miles.* ¹⁷Then he measured the walls and found them to be 216 feet thick* (the angel used a standard human measure).

21:3 Some manuscripts read *God himself will be with them, their God.* **21:10** Or *in the Spirit.* **21:16** Greek *12,000 stadia* [2,220 kilometers]. **21:17** Greek *144 cubits* [65 meters].

21:3
2 Chr 6:18
Ezek 37:27
Zech 2:10
2 Cor 6:16

21:4
Isa 25:8; 35:10;
43:18; 65:19

21:5
Isa 43:19
2 Cor 5:17

21:6
Rev 1:8; 22:13

21:7
2 Sam 7:14
Rom 8:14
2 Cor 6:16

21:8
Ps 5:6
1 Cor 6:9
Eph 5:5

21:9
Rev 15:1, 7; 19:7

21:10
Ezek 40:1-2
Rev 1:10; 17:3

21:11
Isa 60:1-2, 19
Ezek 43:2
Rev 4:3

21:12
Exod 28:21
Ezek 48:30-34
Rev 22:14

21:14
Eph 2:20
Heb 11:10

21:15
Ezek 40:3, 5

21:16-17
Ezek 48:16-17

---

to be with us, just as God became man in Jesus Christ and lived among us (John 1:14). Wherever God reigns, there is peace, security, and love.

• **21:3, 4** Have you ever wondered what eternity will be like? The "holy city, the new Jerusalem" is described as the place where God will "remove all . . . sorrows." Forevermore, there will be no death, sorrow, crying, or pain. What a wonderful truth! No matter what you are going through, it's not the last word—God has written the final chapter, and it is about true fulfillment and eternal joy for those who love him. We do not know as much as we would like, but it is enough to know that eternity with God will be more wonderful than we could ever imagine.

• **21:5** God is the Creator. The Bible begins with the majestic story of his creation of the universe, and it concludes with his creation of a new heaven and a new earth. This is a tremendous hope and encouragement for the believer. When we are with God, with our sins forgiven and our future secure, we will be like Christ. We will be made perfect like him.

21:6 Just as God finished the work of creation (Genesis 2:1-3) and Jesus finished the work of redemption (John 19:30), so the Trinity will finish the entire plan of salvation by inviting the redeemed into a new creation.

21:6 For more about the water of life, see the note on 22:1.

• **21:7, 8** The "cowards" are not those who are fainthearted in their faith or who sometimes doubt or question but those who turn back from following God. They are not brave enough to stand up for Christ; they are not humble enough to accept his authority over their lives. They are put in the same list as the unbelieving, the corrupt, the murderers, the immoral, the idolaters, the liars, and those practicing magic arts.

People who are victorious "endure to the end" (Mark 13:13). They will receive the blessings that God promised: (1) eating from the tree of life (Revelation 2:7), (2) escaping from the lake of fire (the "second death," 2:11), (3) receiving a special name (2:17), (4) having authority over the nations (2:26), (5) being included in the Book of Life (3:5), (6) being a pillar in God's spiritual temple (3:12), and (7) sitting with Christ on his throne (3:21). Those who can endure the testing of evil and remain faithful will be rewarded by God.

21:8 The lake is explained in the notes on 19:20 and 20:14. The second death is spiritual death, meaning either eternal torment or destruction. In either case, it is permanent separation from God.

• **21:10ff** The rest of the chapter is a stunning description of the new city of God. The vision is symbolic and shows us that our new home with God will defy description. We will not be disappointed by it in any way.

• **21:12-14** The new Jerusalem is a picture of God's future home for his people. The 12 tribes of Israel (21:12) probably represent all the faithful in the Old Testament; the 12 apostles (21:14) represent the church. Thus, both believing Gentiles and Jews who have been faithful to God will live together in the new earth.

21:15-17 The city's measurements are symbolic of a place that will hold all God's people. These measurements are all multiples of 12, the number for God's people: There were 12 tribes in Israel, and 12 apostles who started the church. The walls are 144 (12 x 12) cubits (200 feet) thick; There are 12 layers in the walls, and 12 gates in the city; and the height, length, and breadth are all the same, 12,000 stadia (1,400 miles). The new Jerusalem is a perfect cube, the same shape as the Most Holy Place in the Temple (1 Kings 6:20). These measurements illustrate that this new home will be perfect for us.

21:19
Exod 28:17-20
Isa 54:11-12
Ezek 28:13

21:21
Isa 54:12

21:22
John 4:21-24;
17:21-24

21:23
Isa 60:19-20

21:24
Isa 60:3, 5

21:25
Isa 60:11
Zech 14:7

21:27
Isa 52:1

¹⁸ The wall was made of jasper, and the city was pure gold, as clear as glass. ¹⁹ The wall of the city was built on foundation stones inlaid with twelve gems: the first was jasper, the second sapphire, the third agate, the fourth emerald, ²⁰ the fifth onyx, the sixth carnelian, the seventh chrysolite, the eighth beryl, the ninth topaz, the tenth chrysoprase, the eleventh jacinth, the twelfth amethyst.

²¹ The twelve gates were made of pearls—each gate from a single pearl! And the main street was pure gold, as clear as glass.

²² No temple could be seen in the city, for the Lord God Almighty and the Lamb are its temple. ²³ And the city has no need of sun or moon, for the glory of God illuminates the city, and the Lamb is its light. ²⁴ The nations of the earth will walk in its light, and the rulers of the world will come and bring their glory to it. ²⁵ Its gates never close at the end of day because there is no night. ²⁶ And all the nations will bring their glory and honor into the city. ²⁷ Nothing evil will be allowed to enter—no one who practices shameful idolatry and dishonesty—but only those whose names are written in the Lamb's Book of Life.

22:1
Ezek 47:1
Joel 3:18
Zech 14:8
John 7:37-39

22:2
Gen 2:9
Ezek 47:12

22 And the angel showed me a pure river with the water of life, clear as crystal, flowing from the throne of God and of the Lamb, ²coursing down the center of the main street. On each side of the river grew a tree of life, bearing twelve crops of fruit,* with a fresh crop each month. The leaves were used for medicine to heal the nations.

22:2 Or *12 kinds of fruit.*

WHAT WE KNOW ABOUT ETERNITY

Description	Reference
A place prepared for us	John 14:2, 3
Unlimited by physical properties (1 Corinthians 15:35–49)	John 20:19, 26
Like Jesus	1 John 3:2
New bodies	1 Corinthians 15
A wonderful experience	1 Corinthians 2:9
A new environment	Revelation 21:1
A new experience of God's presence (1 Corinthians 13:12)	Revelation 21:3
New emotions	Revelation 21:4
No more death	Revelation 21:4

The Bible devotes much less space to describing eternity than it does to convincing people that eternal life is available as a free gift from God. Most of the brief descriptions of eternity would be more accurately called hints, since they use terms and ideas from present experience to describe what we cannot fully grasp until we are there ourselves. These references hint at aspects of what our future will be like if we have accepted Christ's gift of eternal life.

• **21:18-21** The picture of walls made of jewels reveals that the new Jerusalem will be a place of purity and durability—it will last forever.

• **21:22-24** The Temple, the center of God's presence among his people, was the primary place of worship. No temple is needed in the new city, however, because God's presence will be everywhere. He will be worshiped throughout the city, and nothing will hinder us from being with him.

21:25-27 Not everyone will be allowed into the new Jerusalem, but "only those whose names are written in the Lamb's Book of Life." (The Book of Life is explained in the notes on 3:5 and 20:12-15.) Don't think that you will get in because of your background, personality, or good behavior. Eternal life is available to you only because of what Jesus, the Lamb, has done. Trust him today to secure your citizenship in his new creation.

22:1 The water of life is a symbol of eternal life. Jesus used this same image with the Samaritan woman (John 4:7-14). It pictures the fullness of life with God and the eternal blessings that come when we believe in him and allow him to satisfy our spiritual thirst (see 22:17).

• **22:2** This tree of life is like the tree of life in the Garden of Eden (Genesis 2:9). After Adam and Eve sinned, they were forbidden to eat from the tree of life because they could not have eternal life as long as they were under sin's control. But because of the forgiveness of sin through the blood of Jesus, there will be no evil or sin in this city. We will be able to eat freely from the tree of life when sin's control over us is destroyed and our eternity with God is secure.

22:2 Why would the nations need to be healed if all evil is gone? John is quoting from Ezekiel 47:12, where water flowing from the Temple produces trees with healing leaves. He is not implying that there will be illness in the new earth; he is emphasizing that the water of life produces health and strength wherever it goes.

³No longer will anything be cursed. For the throne of God and of the Lamb will be there, and his servants will worship him. ⁴And they will see his face, and his name will be written on their foreheads. ⁵And there will be no night there—no need for lamps or sun—for the Lord God will shine on them. And they will reign forever and ever.

⁶Then the angel said to me, "These words are trustworthy and true: 'The Lord God, who tells his prophets what the future holds, has sent his angel to tell you what will happen soon.'"

Jesus Is Coming

⁷" Look, I am coming soon! Blessed are those who obey the prophecy written in this scroll."

⁸I, John, am the one who saw and heard all these things. And when I saw and heard these things, I fell down to worship the angel who showed them to me. ⁹But again he said, "No, don't worship me. I am a servant of God, just like you and your brothers the prophets, as well as all who obey what is written in this scroll. Worship God!"

¹⁰Then he instructed me, "Do not seal up the prophetic words you have written, for the time is near. ¹¹Let the one who is doing wrong continue to do wrong; the one who is vile, continue to be vile; the one who is good, continue to do good; and the one who is holy, continue in holiness."

¹²" See, I am coming soon, and my reward is with me, to repay all according to their deeds. ¹³I am the Alpha and the Omega, the First and the Last, the Beginning and the End."

¹⁴Blessed are those who wash their robes so they can enter through the gates of the city and eat the fruit from the tree of life. ¹⁵Outside the city are the dogs—the sorcerers, the sexually immoral, the murderers, the idol worshipers, and all who love to live a lie.

¹⁶" I, Jesus, have sent my angel to give you this message for the churches. I am both the source of David and the heir to his throne.* I am the bright morning star."

¹⁷The Spirit and the bride say, "Come." Let each one who hears them say, "Come."

22:16 Greek *I am the root and offspring of David.*

Cross-references (margin):

22:3 Zech 14:11
22:4 Pss 17:15; 42:2; Matt 5:8
22:5 Isa 60:19-20; Dan 7:18, 27; Zech 14:7
22:8 1 Jn 1:1-3
22:11 Ezek 3:27; Dan 12:10
22:12 Matt 16:27
22:13 Rev 1:8, 17; 21:6
22:14 Gen 2:9; 3:22; Ezek 47:12; Rev 2:7; 21:12, 27
22:15 1 Cor 6:9-10; Gal 5:19-21; Rev 21:8
22:16 Num 24:17; Isa 11:1, 10; Matt 1:1; Rom 1:3
22:17 Isa 55:1; John 7:37-39

22:3 "No longer will anything be cursed" means that nothing accursed will be in God's presence. This fulfills Zechariah's prophecy (see Zechariah 14:11).

22:8, 9 Hearing or reading an eyewitness account is the next best thing to seeing the event yourself. John witnessed the events reported in Revelation and wrote them down so we could see and believe as he did. If you have read this far, you have seen. Have you also believed?

• **22:8, 9** The first of the Ten Commandments is "Do not worship any other gods besides me" (Exodus 20:3). Jesus said that the greatest command of Moses' laws was "You must love the Lord your God with all your heart, all your soul, and all your mind" (Matthew 22:37). Here, at the end of the Bible, this truth is reiterated. The angel instructs John to "worship God!" God alone is worthy of our worship and adoration. He is above all creation, even the angels. Are there people, ideas, goals, or possessions that occupy the central place in your life, crowding God out? Worship *only* God by allowing nothing to distract you from your devotion to him.

• **22:10, 11** The angel tells John what to do after his vision is over. Instead of sealing up what he has written, as Daniel was commanded to do (Daniel 12:4-12), the book is to be left open so that all can read and understand. Daniel's message was sealed because it was not a message for Daniel's time. But the book of Revelation was a message for John's time, and it is relevant today. As Christ's return gets closer, there is a greater polarization between God's followers and Satan's followers. We must read the book of Revelation, hear its message, and be prepared for Christ's imminent return.

• **22:12-14** Those who wash their robes are those who seek to purify themselves from a sinful way of life. They strive daily to remain faithful and ready for Christ's return. This concept is also explained in the second note on 7:14.

22:14 In Eden, Adam and Eve were barred from any access to the tree of life because of their sin (Genesis 3:22-24). In the new earth, God's people will eat from the tree of life because their sins have been removed by Christ's death and resurrection. Those who eat the fruit of this tree will live forever. If Jesus has forgiven your sins, you will have the right to eat from this tree. For more on this concept, see the first note on 22:2.

22:15 The exact location of these sinners is not known, nor is it relevant. They are outside. They were judged and condemned in 21:8. The emphasis is that nothing evil and no sinner will be in God's presence to corrupt or harm any of the faithful.

22:16 Jesus is both David's "source" and "heir." As the Creator of all, Jesus existed long before David. As a human, however, he was one of David's direct descendants (see Isaiah 11:1-5; Matthew 1:1-17). As the Messiah, he is the "bright morning star," the light of salvation to all.

• **22:17** Both the Holy Spirit and the bride, the church, extend the invitation to all the world to come to Jesus and experience the joys of salvation in Christ.

• **22:17** When Jesus met the Samaritan woman at the well, he told her of the living water that he could supply (John 4:10-15). This image is used again as Christ invites anyone to come and drink of the water of life. The Good News is unlimited in scope—all people everywhere may come. Salvation cannot be earned, but God gives it freely. We live in a world desperately thirsty for living water, and many are dying of thirst. But it's still not too late. Let us invite everyone to come and drink.

22:18
Deut 4:2; 12:32
Prov 30:6
Rev 15:6–16:21

22:19
Gen 2:9; 3:22
Ezek 47:12
Rev 2:7; 22:14

22:20
1 Cor 16:22

22:21
Rom 16:20
2 Thes 3:18

Let the thirsty ones come—anyone who wants to. Let them come and drink the water of life without charge. ¹⁸And I solemnly declare to everyone who hears the prophetic words of this book: If anyone adds anything to what is written here, God will add to that person the plagues described in this book. ¹⁹And if anyone removes any of the words of this prophetic book, God will remove that person's share in the tree of life and in the holy city that are described in this book.

²⁰He who is the faithful witness to all these things says, " Yes, I am coming soon!" Amen! Come, Lord Jesus!

²¹The grace of the Lord Jesus be with you all.

- **22:18, 19** This warning is given to those who might purposefully distort the message in this book. Moses gave a similar warning in Deuteronomy 4:1-4. We, too, must handle the Bible with care and great respect so that we do not distort its message, even unintentionally. We should be quick to put its principles into practice in our life. No human explanation or interpretation of God's Word should be elevated to the same authority as the text itself.

- **22:20** We don't know the day or the hour, but Jesus is coming soon and unexpectedly. This is good news to those who trust him, but a terrible message for those who have rejected him and stand under judgment. *Soon* means "at any moment," and we must be ready for him, always prepared for his return. Would Jesus' sudden appearance catch you off guard?

- **22:21** Revelation closes human history as Genesis opened it— in paradise. But there is one distinct difference in Revelation— evil is gone forever. Genesis describes Adam and Eve walking and talking with God; Revelation describes people worshiping

God face to face. Genesis describes a garden with an evil serpent; Revelation describes a perfect city with no evil. The Garden of Eden was destroyed by sin; but paradise is re-created in the new Jerusalem.

The book of Revelation ends with an urgent plea: "Come, Lord Jesus!" In a world of problems, persecution, evil, and immorality, Christ calls us to endure in our faith. Our efforts to better our world are important, but their results cannot compare with the transformation that Jesus will bring about when he returns. He alone controls human history, forgives sin, and will re-create the earth and bring lasting peace.

Revelation is, above all, a book of hope. It shows that no matter what happens on earth, God is in control. It promises that evil will not last forever. And it depicts the wonderful reward that is waiting for all those who believe in Jesus Christ as Savior and Lord.

STUDY QUESTIONS

Thirteen lessons for individual or group study

It's always exciting to get more than you expect. And that's what you'll find in this Bible study guide—much more than you expect. Our goal was to write thoughtful, practical, dependable, and application-oriented studies of God's Word.

This study guide contains the complete text of the selected Bible book. The commentary is accurate, complete, and loaded with unique charts, maps, and profiles of Bible people.

With the Bible text, extensive notes and helps, and questions to guide discussion, these Life Application Study Guides have everything you need in one place.

The lessons in this Bible study guide will work for large classes as well as small-group studies. To get everyone involved in your discussions, encourage participants to answer the questions before each meeting.

Each lesson is divided into five easy-to-lead sections. The section called "Reflect" introduces you and the members of your group to a specific area of life touched by the lesson. "Read" shows which chapters to read and which notes and other features to use. Additional questions help you understand the passage. "Realize" brings into focus the biblical principle to be learned with questions, a special insight, or both. "Respond" helps you make connections with your own situation and personal needs. The questions are designed to help you find areas in your life where you can apply the biblical truths. "Resolve" helps you map out action plans for that day.

Begin and end each lesson with prayer, asking for the Holy Spirit's guidance, direction, and wisdom.

Recommended time allotments for each section of a lesson are as follows:

Segment	**60 minutes**	**90 minutes**
Reflect on your life	5 minutes	10 minutes
Read the passage	10 minutes	15 minutes
Realize the principle	15 minutes	20 minutes
Respond to the message	20 minutes	30 minutes
Resolve to take action	10 minutes	15 minutes

All five sections work together to help a person learn the lessons, live out the principles, and obey the commands taught in the Bible.

Also, at the end of each lesson, there is a section entitled "More for studying other themes in this section." These questions will help you lead the group in studying other parts of each section not covered in depth by the main lesson.

And remember, it is a message to obey, not just to listen to. If you don't obey, you are only fooling yourself. For if you just listen and don't obey, it is like looking at your face in a mirror but doing nothing to improve your appearance. You see yourself, walk away, and forget what you look like. But if you keep looking steadily into God's perfect law—the law that sets you free—and if you do what it says and don't forget what you heard, then God will bless you for doing it. (James 1:22–25)

REFLECT
on your life

1 List a number of warning signs that you might encounter in a given week.

_____

_____

2 List some signs of hope. What is it about these signs that encourages you?

_____

_____

3 Think of the places in the world where Christians face persecution today. If you could offer one message that would encourage them, what would you say?

_____

_____

_____

READ
the passage

Read the two-page Introduction to Revelation and the following charts: "Interpreting the Book of Revelation" (chapter 1), "A Journey through the Book of Revelation (chapter 2)," "Events in Revelation Described Elsewhere in the Bible" (chapter 5), and "The Beginning and the End" (chapter 21). Also read the following notes:

❐ 1:1   ❐ 1:1–3   ❐ 1:3

4 The Introduction describes this book as apocalyptic literature. What does that mean, and why would this type of book be difficult for most people to understand?

_____

_____

_____

_____

5 The word *apocalyptic* means "unveiling, disclosure, or revelation." What is being unveiled, and why is it important that God is the one who takes the initiative in doing this?

_____

_____

_____

_____

6 What kinds of hardships have you faced? How do your hardships compare with the disaster and oppression described in Revelation?

_____

_____

_____

_____

_____

_____

REALIZE the principle

This book brings a message of warning and hope for men and women of every generation. To those undergoing persecution, being stretched in their faith, or wondering if the battle against the evil in this world really will be won, Revelation brings comfort and hope. God will triumph! Christ will return and set things straight. But Revelation warns those who would take God for granted or neglect their faith. Judgment is sure! Be ready!

7 In the process of following Christ, hope encourages movement, and warning provides direction. Read the following Megathemes in the Introduction. Then write down how each would provide hope and warning.

Megatheme	Hope	Warning
God's Sovereignty	_____	_____
	_____	_____
Christ's Return	_____	_____
	_____	_____
God's Faithful People	_____	Devoted only to Christ

RESPOND
to the message

Thos who refuse to believe eternal punishment   _Evil & injustice will not prevail_

8 How does God warn people today? What is he warning Christians about today?

Through His Word
Not to lose faith
Don't be led astray by nonbelievers

9 Imagine you learned God was going to stop warning us about evil and start executing judgment tomorrow morning. What would you do?

PRAY! Repent
Try to bring others to Christ before the end

10 On what do people pin their hopes today?

money
material things

11 What are some of the ways God fills you with hope? Where do you feel the need for hope in your life right now?

RESOLVE
to take action

12 Write down one truth about God that has given you hope. Then write a prayer of thanksgiving for that truth.

_____

_____

_____

_____

13 Identify one warning God has given you in the past few weeks. How has that affected the direction of your life? List several changes that the warning has caused you to make.

_____ MORE
_____ for studying
_____ other themes
                                                  in this section
_____

_____

A Why was the letter about God's triumph over evil so timely for the churches at the end of the first century? Why is it still timely today? Why is it meaningful to every generation?

B Which of the four main interpretative approaches in the chart "Interpreting the Book of Revelation" is the closest to how you understand this book? Which ones are entirely new to you?

C Look up all the events in the chart "Events in Revelation Described Elsewhere in the Bible." What conclusions can you draw about the unity and continuity of the Bible?

D Compare and contrast the Gospel of John and the book of Revelation.

E In what ways was John specially prepared to receive this revelation and write it down?

LESSON 2
FACE TO FACE WITH CHRIST
REVELATION 1:1–20

REFLECT
on your life

1 Suppose you were to introduce Jesus Christ to a group. What would you say about him? What would you include in your description of him?

_____

_____

_____

2 List all the names you can think of that the Bible gives to Jesus Christ. What does each name convey or reveal about Christ?

_____

_____

_____

READ
the passage

Read Revelation 1:1–20, the chart "The Names of Jesus" (chapter 2), and the following notes:

❐ 1:5, 6   ❐ 1:5–7   ❐ 1:8   ❐ 1:9   ❐ 1:12, 13   ❐ 1:17, 18

3 Describe how each name for Jesus in this passage affects believers.

_____

_____

_____

_____

_____

_____

_____

_____

_____

4 John details eight characteristics of Christ's appearance in verses 13–16. List these characteristics and what each represents.

_____

_____

_____

_____

_____

_____

_____

_____

_____

5 John is described in the Gospels as one of the three apostles who enjoyed a special relationship with Jesus. Of all the apostles, he was probably the closest to Jesus. How could John know Jesus so well and yet be awed by him?

The more you know of Jesus
the more you should be awed

REALIZE
the principle

_____

_____

_____

Revelation describes a vision of our risen and powerful Lord. Meeting Christ might be an anxious experience for some; others might even decline if they had the opportunity. And yet one day we all will see him face to face, when he returns or when we die. It would be tragic for you to be unprepared, having neglected him during your lifetime. What do you need to do now to be ready to meet Christ?

6 The vision of Jesus shows us how he works in our life. Jesus walks among the lampstands (1:13) in a way similar to the way he works in the church. At the time, John was the one responsible for the churches named in Revelation. How would this vision of Jesus have affected John's attitude as he cared for the church?

_____

_____

_____

_____

_____

7 John was also facing a time of persecution. He was in exile on the island of Patmos. How do times of persecution affect a person's attitude and outlook on life? How would the presence of Jesus, as he is seen here, affect the depression and disappointment felt by an exile?

_____

_____

_____

RESPOND
to the message

8 How does Jesus make his presence felt in your life?

_____

_____

_____

_____

9 How is he moving through your life with awesome majesty?

_____

_____

_____

_____

10 This vision came as a surprise to John. How has Jesus surprised you lately? Why does he move in your life when you least expect it?

_____

_____

_____

RESOLVE
to take action

11 Which of Jesus' titles mentioned in this chapter is most meaningful to you? Which do you most need to keep in mind? What can you do to keep these characteristics of Jesus in mind as you go through your week?

_____

_____

_____

_____

A What is the blessing referred to in 1:3? How does it apply to our churches today?

MORE
for studying
other themes
in this section

B Why was this originally addressed to the seven churches in the province of Asia rather than all Christians everywhere?

C What does the appearance of Jesus tell us about his character and nature?

D How is this vision similar to and different from those received by prophets in the Old Testament?

E What attribute of Christ are you most grateful for? Select one, and express your gratitude for that attribute each day for one week.

LESSON 3
GETTING A COMPLETE PHYSICAL
REVELATION 2:1—3:22

1 What junk mail do you resent the most?

REFLECT
on your life

_____

_____

_____

2 You just received a letter in the mail with the following warning written on the envelope: "Inside is written your most important secret." Describe your reaction as you take the envelope in hand. What would you do? Would you open it? burn it? hide it?

_____

_____

_____

_____

_____

Read Revelation 2:1—3:22 and the following notes:

❏ 1:4 ❏ 2:1ff ❏ 2:5 ❏ 2:6 ❏ 2:13 ❏ 2:14 ❏ 3:10 ❏ 3:15, 16 ❏ 3:19

READ
the passage

3 As Jesus addressed each church, he told the people something about themselves that they already knew (that they were under pressure, that they were well-off, etc.). But then he pointed out something that probably surprised or shocked them. Read about each church. Then list what you think they already knew and what came as a surprise.

	They knew they were:	*They were surprised to be:*
Ephesus	_____	_____
Smyrna	_____	_____
Pergamum	_____	_____
Thyatira	_____	_____
Sardis	_____	_____
Philadelphia	_____	_____
Laodicea	_____	_____

4 This letter was to be read when the church was gathered together. If you had been in one of these churches, what would you want to say at the next congregational meeting?

_____

_____

_____

_____

_____

_____

Christ walks among the churches and evaluates them openly and honestly. In each situation, he promises that he will come to them in person (2:5, 16, 25; 3:5, 11, 20). Undoubtedly this kind of message would shake up the church leaders, especially where the evaluation was negative. The truth is, however, that Christ is walking among us today, evaluating our devotion and obedience to him. How do you think he views your church? your life? What kind of a letter would he write to you?

REALIZE
the principle

5 Each of the seven letters is addressed to the church as a congregation, but in each letter the invitation to change is very personal. How do the sins of others affect your life, fellowship, and reputation?

_____

_____

_____

_____

_____

_____

6 Jesus says, "Anyone who is willing to hear should listen." What effect can there be on a group when one person decides to make the changes God wants?

_____

_____

_____

_____

RESPOND
to the message

7 Notice how some of the churches had accommodated themselves to the sin around them. How do Christians often rationalize their own weaknesses, failings, and shortcomings?

_____

_____

_____

_____

_____

_____

8 How do your actions affect the failure or success of your church or fellowship group?

_____

_____

_____

_____

_____

9 If Jesus were to write a letter to you, what would you be afraid he might mention?

_____

_____

_____

_____

_____

10 Use the pattern of these letters as described in the note labeled 2:1ff and write a letter to your *own* congregation. Include at least one item of commendation and one item that would require correction. Look at that letter and add at least three actions you could take (personally or with a few others) to head the church in that direction.

RESOLVE
to take action

_____

_____

_____

_____

_____

_____

_____

_____

_____

_____

A Consider the position of authority Jesus has over the church. How should that affect church leaders as they view their own responsibility?

MORE
for studying
other themes
in this section

B Christ is more concerned about how you relate to him than what you do for him. How is this truth reflected in the attitude of these churches and in our efforts in ministry?

C Define the seven ways Christ identifies himself to the churches. How does each definition match the need of that church? What part of his character would your church need to experience the most?

D What similarities in form do you see among all these letters?

LESSON 4
STEERING CLEAR OF EVIL INFLUENCES
REVELATION 2:1—3:22

REFLECT
on your life

1 List influences in your culture that affect you the most (television, videos, etc.). How do they affect your relationship with Jesus Christ?

_____

_____

_____

_____

_____

READ
the passage

Read Revelation 2:1—3:22 (the same section as the previous lesson) and the following notes:

❒ 2:2   ❒ 2:2, 3   ❒ 2:4   ❒ 2:4, 5   ❒ 2:6   ❒ 2:20   ❒ 3:3   ❒ 3:11   ❒ 3:17

❒ 3:20   ❒ 3:22

2 With each church Jesus is like a doctor looking for a critical illness. He makes a diagnosis and prescribes a cure. Read each letter. Then name the illness Jesus discovered and describe the cure:

	Illness	*Cure*
Ephesus	_____	_____
Smyrna	_____	_____
Pergamum	_____	_____
Thyatira	_____	_____
Sardis	_____	_____
Philadelphia	_____	_____
Laodicea	_____	_____

3 Five of the churches were experiencing serious internal problems. Where did problems like those begin, and how did they develop?

_____

_____

_____

4 Two of the churches were healthy but under pressure. What are some of the positive and negative consequences of pressure on people? on the life of a church?

_____

_____

_____

_____

_____

Christ walks among the churches and gives each one a strong message. Many of the churches were influenced by their culture, becoming indifferent to following Christ, dabbling in immorality, or following false teachers. It is easy to think of a church as an institution or a building, but churches are made up of individuals, of people. The lessons for the churches, therefore, apply to us. What are your trouble spots? What is your spiritual illness?

REALIZE
the principle

5 Two themes are woven together in these letters: love and purity. Why is it important to keep these two connected?

_____

_____

_____

_____

_____

6 What causes love for God to cool?

_____

_____

_____

_____

_____

7 Why is sexual immorality such a concern to God?

_____

_____

_____

_____

_____

8 How are Christians tempted to cut corners in ethics and morality?

_____

_____

_____

_____

_____

RESPOND
to the message

9 What have you encountered that tempts you to move away from Christ?

_____

_____

_____

_____

10 If you have found yourself tempted by impurity, what steps have helped you deal with it effectively?

_____

_____

_____

_____

11 Of all the potential dangers identified in these churches, with which do you find it the most difficult to deal?

_____

_____

_____

_____

12 Choose one influence in your world that affects your love relationship with God (e.g., television, sports, work, etc.). What is it about that influence that is so dangerous? What changes should you make? Write down several steps you can take to correct its influence on you.

RESOLVE
to take action

_____

_____

_____

_____

_____

A How is a life of faith affected by material possessions? What are spiritual riches?

B Consider the contrast between reputation and reality. What dangers are there for people who spend time cultivating their image instead of their character?

C What types of evil influences were these churches exposed to in Asia Minor?

D Who were the Nicolaitans? How are similar influences felt in our churches today?

MORE
for studying
other themes
in this section

L E S S O N 5
WORSHIP HIS MAJESTY
REVELATION 4:1—5:14

1 Think back to a very meaningful worship service. What about the service affected and impressed you the most?

REFLECT
on your life

_____

_____

_____

_____

_____

Read Revelation 4:1—5:14 and the following notes:

❏ 4:4 ❏ 4:6, 7 ❏ 4:11 ❏ 5:5 ❏ 5:5, 6 ❏ 5:9, 10 ❏ 5:10

READ
the passage

2 Consider the setting of the worship service described in this passage. What is there about this scene that might impact our own worship services?

_____

_____

_____

_____

3 The word *worship* literally means "to attribute worth to God." List the actions and attributes of God described in chapter 4 that explain how worthy he is.

_____

_____

_____

_____

_____

4 How do you think John reacted to all he saw and heard?

_____

_____

_____

In this section, God the Father and God the Son appear in all their majesty. Their true identity is revealed. And the response of all living creatures is to fall down and worship in reverence, awe, and submission. Their worship includes giving praise, honor, and glory to almighty God. Today, worship services abound. If God is truly present when we worship, how do we show humility and praise? Is anything missing from your worship?

REALIZE
the principle

5 In chapter 4 it is obvious that God's authority is absolute. In chapter 5 the attention shifts to Jesus Christ. What does this say about Christ's place in our life and our world?

_____

_____

_____

_____

_____

6 Why did John weep in 5:4 when no one was found worthy enough to open the scroll?

_____

_____

_____

7 What made Jesus the only one worthy to open the scroll?

_____

_____

_____

8 How would this vision of God on his throne change John's life?

_____

_____

_____

RESPOND
to the message

9 How worshipful are the worship services at your church?

_____

_____

_____

_____

10 What kinds of changes would help you worship better? What is the proper way to suggest or to make these changes?

_____

_____

_____

_____

_____

11 When you participate in worship, what do you do reasonably well?

_____

_____

_____

_____

_____

12 How could discipline help you in your worship of God?

_____

_____

_____

_____

_____

13 Notice that the songs sung in this service begin with heavenly beings and end with human choirs. Those who know God best are teaching others how to worship by attributing worth to God. How did you learn to worship?

_____

_____

_____

_____

14 Approach your next worship service as an explorer. As you listen to the songs and follow through the service, keep a list of the attributes (aspects of God's character) that you discover. Then write down how you have experienced God's attributes in your life, and praise him for this.

RESOLVE
to take action

_____

_____

_____

_____

_____

A As he is worshiped, Jesus is called both a Lion and a Lamb. How are both accurate descriptions of Christ? If we are to be like him, what does this say about the way we exercise strength and meekness?

MORE
for studying
other themes
in this section

B Read the three songs, and compare the three different groups. What do they teach us about Christ?

C Consider the relationship of God's holiness and this scene of incredible majesty as it relates to the upcoming judgments. What is the relationship between God's holiness and justice? How should we respond to God's holiness? How should the truth of his justice and judgment change your life?

D How can Christ be pictured both as a Lion and as a Lamb?

LESSON 6
PREPARING FOR PERSECUTION
REVELATION 6:1—8:5

REFLECT
on your life

1 Think back to when you received something you knew you deserved but didn't expect to receive—like a traffic ticket for going five miles per hour over the speed limit on a familiar stretch of road. How did you feel?

_____

_____

_____

2 What is the worst thing that has happened to you because of your relationship with Jesus Christ? How have you suffered for him?

_____

_____

_____

READ
the passage

Read Revelation 6:1—8:5 and the following notes:

❏ 6:1ff ❏ 6:2–8 ❏ 6:9 ❏ 6:9–11 ❏ 6:15–17 ❏ 7:2 ❏ 7:3 ❏ 7:9 ❏ 7:14

❏ 7:16, 17 ❏ 7:17

3 There are two groups of people identified in these chapters: those who do not belong to God (6:15–17) and those who belong to him (chapter 7). What is the difference in their reactions to everything that God has been doing?

_____

_____

_____

_____

4 Listen to the message of the fifth angel (7:2, 3). What does it mean to be sealed? Who benefits from the process?

_____

_____

_____

_____

Sometimes we make the mistake of thinking that God owes us a better life. That was the attitude of the people who asked Jesus why some "innocent" people had died (Luke 13:1). Instead of apologizing, Jesus said, "And you will also perish unless you turn from your evil ways and turn to God." They were asking the wrong question. We also ask the wrong question when we ask God why we experience hardships. In a sinful world, the right question is not "Why is there suffering?" but "Why don't I suffer more?"

**REALIZE
the principle**

5 From his perspective, John sees that God controls the whole process and is able to take care of his own people. How does that perspective affect someone who is facing extreme pressure?

_____

_____

_____

_____

6 What conditions allow the vast crowd of 7:9 to wear their robes and sing their songs? What is it about God that they have learned from their experience?

_____

_____

_____

_____

7 The message of the angel in 7:14 is that suffering has a purifying effect. What does God use to purify our faith? How do we usually respond to this purifying process?

_____

_____

_____

_____

RESPOND
to the message

8 What are some of the ways Christians try to explain tragedy?

_____

_____

_____

_____

_____

9 Think again of the most difficult situation you have had to face because of your faith in Christ (see question 2). How did it affect your relationship with him?

_____

_____

_____

_____

10 What would happen in your life and in your church's life if persecution were to break out in your community?

_____

_____

_____

_____

11 How would persecution affect your relationship with God?

_____

_____

_____

_____

12 If you were on a vacation or a business trip in another country and were arrested for being a Christian, what would frighten you most about the possibility of persecution or even martyrdom?

_____

_____

_____

_____

13 How would you need to change in order to be better prepared for persecution, imprisonment, and possibly death for the sake of Christ?

_____

_____

_____

_____

14 Imagine that you find out you will be persecuted for your faith tomorrow. Write down the changes you need to make today. What could you do to encourage or help others?

RESOLVE
to take action

_____

_____

_____

_____

A The four horses and riders of chapter 6 represent victory, war, famine, and death. Consider how each one leads to the other. What example can you give of this pattern from what you know of current events?

MORE
for studying
other themes
in this section

B Read the study notes on 7:10 and 7:14 and consider the dynamics behind salvation. How is salvation described as a free gift, and how is it nurtured in your life?

C How does the description in 8:1–4 help us understand and picture what happens when we pray?

REFLECT
on your life

1 What are some of the major evils in your community? What are Christians doing to combat them?

_____

_____

_____

_____

_____

_____

READ
the passage

Read Revelation 8:6—11:19 and the following notes:

❑ 8:6 ❑ 8:7–12 ❑ 8:13 ❑ 9:20, 21 ❑ 10:4 ❑ 11:3 ❑ 11:10 ❑ 11:18

2 Who inflicts the disasters recorded in chapters 8 and 9? How is their power limited? Who limits them?

_____

_____

_____

3 Who are the primary targets of these disasters?

_____

_____

_____

4 How does the world react to the two witnesses (chapter 11)? What is it about God and his holiness that cause people to hate him? What sort of responses do you receive when you witness?

_____

_____

_____

_____

_____

_____

5 At the end of chapter 11, what attribute of God is being praised? What does this praise reveal about God's power and the way he has acted as recorded in chapters 8—11?

REALIZE
the principle

_____

_____

_____

_____

The seven angels sound the trumpets one at a time, and God's terrible judgment begins. In the midst of judgment, however, two witnesses arise, standing against evil and for righteousness. They are killed, and the evil world rejoices. The truth is that humankind loves sin and hates God. And when we speak out for God's power and love, the world hates us. Eventually, however, God will come as judge, eradicating sin and punishing evildoers. Until that day, we must stand firm against evil, despite opposition and persecution, knowing that God's justice will prevail and we will be saved.

6 What is God's purpose for sending these disasters? Does the human response surprise you, or is it something you would have expected? Why?

_____

_____

_____

_____

7 What instruments does God use to get people's attention?

_____

_____

_____

8 God has chosen to use people to be his witnesses and attention-getters in the world. Consider the reaction of the people to the two witnesses. Why would people respond that way to them? How do people react to you when you stand against evil or talk about Christ?

_____

_____

_____

_____

_____

RESPOND
to the message

9 When God points out sin in your life, how should you respond?

_____

_____

_____

_____

_____

10 When God calls us to point out sin in the life of another person, how should we proceed?

_____

_____

_____

_____

_____

RESOLVE
to take action

11 What are some evils in your community against which your church can take a stand? What can you do to help your church get started?

_____

_____

_____

_____

_____

A How does bitterness affect a person's ability to respond to God (8:11)? What is the best way to deal with hardness and bitterness in a person's heart?

B The study note on 11:3 calls to mind the episode in Exodus where God sent plagues on Egypt. In what way are those plagues similar to the ones in this passage? In Exodus, the plagues were designed to change Pharaoh's heart. Because Pharaoh's heart was hard, the Egyptian people had to face all the plagues. What does it take to change a hard heart?

C Consider the reaction people have to the holiness of God. Why would his presence be so intimidating to them? How would that make Christianity seem repulsive to some people?

D Jesus promised his disciples that the world would be hostile to them because it was hostile to him. How does that help to explain the trouble Christians face in the world? What would you say to a Christian who would hide his or her faith because of the world's opposition? For what nonspiritual reasons do Christians generate hostility from the world?

MORE
for studying
other themes
in this section

LESSON 8
CAUGHT IN THE CROSSFIRE
REVELATION 12:1—14:20

1 Describe the worst conflict you have ever been involved in.

_____

_____

_____

2 Why does becoming a Christian or growing in faith sometimes bring more conflict into a person's life?

_____

_____

_____

Read Revelation 12:1—14:20 and the following notes:

❐ 12:1—14:20 ❐ 12:1–6 ❐ 12:6 ❐ 12:12 ❐ 12:17 ❐ 13:1ff ❐ 13:7

❐ 13:11ff ❐ 13:16–18 ❐ 14:1ff ❐ 14:6, 7 ❐ 14:9–11 ❐ 14:13 ❐ 14:14–16

3 What does the warfare between the dragon and the woman in chapter 12 say about the conflict between Satan and the people of God? What would explain the fury behind Satan's pursuit?

_____

_____

_____

4 The beast out of the sea represents political power. What impact does he have on believers? How can political systems test believers' allegiance?

_____

_____

_____

_____

5 The beast out of the earth represents religious but not necessarily Christian authority. Again, what impact does he have on believers? How can the exercise of religious authority challenge believers' allegiance to God?

_____

_____

_____

_____

6 Contrast Satan's message and methods in chapter 13 with God's system in chapter 14. How does Satan try to counterfeit what God does? How successful is he?

_____

_____

_____

_____

7 How is death explained in 14:13? How does that explanation help those who are crushed under the weight of conflict?

_____

_____

_____

_____

The great and wondrous sign of the woman and the dragon shows us the mighty force of the conflict between good and evil. This may seem far removed from us until we realize that much of the daily conflict we experience reflects the much larger conflict of Christ against Satan. Being for Christ places us against the evil system of this world. Taking a stand for Christ against evil puts us on the front lines of battle in this war. In a sense, we are caught in the crossfire. Our duty is to have faith, stand against sin, worship God, and endure.

REALIZE
the principle

8 What is the source of comfort for those who have gone through the chaos of chapters 12 and 13 (see 14:1–5)? How does this give hope to believers who are experiencing intense conflict?

_____

_____

_____

9 What are the areas of greatest conflict in your life? Which of these can be reduced or resolved without diminishing your faith?

RESPOND
to the message

_____

_____

_____

10 In what areas should you be in conflict but are not?

_____

_____

_____

11 In which settings does your faith make friends, neighbors, coworkers, or relatives feel uncomfortable? Which of these situations are reflections of the great struggle of good against evil?

_____

_____

_____

12 If we have been saved by Christ, why do we still have conflict in the church?

_____

_____

_____

13 What are some of the ways this conflict is being carried on in your community?

_____

_____

_____

14 How should Christians protect themselves from the opposition of the evil forces in this world?

_____

_____

_____

15 In what ways are you facing conflict with evil? What kind of reinforcements do you need to withstand this pressure? How can others help you to endure and remain faithful?

RESOLVE
to take action

_____

_____

_____

A What is the difference between physical and spiritual protection? How does God protect us? How does he prepare and compensate believers for physical damage (12:6; 13:5–7; 13:10)?

MORE
for studying
other themes
in this section

B Why does talking about death make us feel uncomfortable? How might this section of Scripture prepare believers to face death? How might it comfort them?

C What do you fear the most about death? What are you doing to prepare for your death?

D Review the symbolism in 13:16–18, specifically the number 666. How is this number a feeble attempt by Satan to imitate God?

E Evaluate the message of the eternal gospel given by the angel (14:6, 7). Who carries such a message today? How are you carrying that message? Is the message of the eternal gospel taken as good or bad news by those who hear it? What does the following message of doom (14:8-11) say to those who reject the gospel?

F Rate your level of spiritual endurance. What do you need to strengthen your confidence? What is there in 14:11, 12 that would give you strength?

G What is it about spiritual warfare that seems the most real to you? Where do you see Satan's fury unleashed against God's people?

H Contrast the use of power by the dragon and two beasts with the use of power by the three angels. What is the role of preaching and proclamation in this great conflict?

REFLECT
on your life

1 What gets you really angry? What do you do when you get angry? What does it take to calm you down?

_____

_____

_____

2 What are some of the deadlines you face in life? What do you do when you can't make a deadline?

_____

_____

_____

READ
the passage

Read Revelation 15:1—16:21 and the following notes:

❏ 15:1   ❏ 15:5–8   ❏ 16:1ff   ❏ 16:7   ❏ 16:9–21   ❏ 16:15   ❏ 16:16

3 Chapter 15 describes God's holiness. How does God's holiness relate to his wrath?

_____

_____

_____

_____

4 Review the acts of worship recorded in chapter 15. Why is God praised? Who offers this praise?

_____

_____

_____

5 How does the judgment of the bowls differ in speed and totality from the seals and the trumpets?

_____

_____

_____

_____

This is the third in the series of judgments. The seals and trumpets lead into this scene of wrath. God's wrath was not eliminated when Jesus died on the cross, nor will it diminish over time. We should take his wrath as seriously as we do his love. We will not find a way out by what we do. It is because of Christ and through him alone that we escape God's wrath.

REALIZE
the principle

6 God is described elsewhere in the Bible as being loving and here as being wrathful. How is it possible to be both? How does his holiness help to explain both?

_____

_____

_____

_____

_____

_____

7 Although these are final judgments, John points out that there was an opportunity for the people to respond to God (16:9, 11, 21). What was their response? What should have been their response?

_____

_____

_____

_____

_____

8 How many chances has God given humankind to repent? How many chances do you think he needs to give?

_____

_____

_____

_____

_____

_____

RESPOND
to the message

9 How do you tend to emphasize God's love and ignore his wrath? What does that do to your understanding of God?

_____

_____

_____

_____

_____

10 What might you say to someone who says that God is too loving to punish the people he created?

_____

_____

_____

_____

_____

11 How many opportunities has God given you to repent? Why did he give you more than one opportunity?

_____

_____

_____

_____

12 Write down something about your thinking, relationships, or behavior of which you are sure God does not approve. Review in your mind the times you have sensed his warning but have ignored him. Then thank him for his kindness, ask his forgiveness for ignoring him each time, and ask his help in putting this sin out of your life.

RESOLVE
to take action

_____

_____

_____

_____

_____

A Compare the song in chapter 15 with Moses' song in Exodus 15:1–18 (see the notes in chapter 15). What are some of the conditions that rule worship? What allows you to praise God for his awesome acts in your life?

MORE
for studying
other themes
in this section

B When we read Psalm 119:137, we acknowledge that God's judgments are righteous and that we agree with them. How would you respond to his judgments if you were to see them as you do in Revelation 16? What makes the difference?

C Why does Christ compare himself to a thief? Why is the fact of his sudden return important?

D How could people be so evil and insensible as to not repent after experiencing these judgments? What might it take to turn someone to God?

LESSON 10
THE EVIL SYSTEM OF THIS WORLD
REVELATION 17:1—18:24

REFLECT
on your life

1 List five of the world's richest and most famous individuals. Why are they well known?

_____

_____

_____

_____

2 Describe the most impressive city you have ever visited.

_____

_____

_____

_____

READ
the passage

Read Revelation 17:1—18:24, the chart "How Can a Person Keep Away from the Evil System?" and the following notes:

❏ 17:1ff ❏ 17:6 ❏ 17:12 ❏ 17:16 ❏ 17:17 ❏ 18:1ff ❏ 18:2, 3 ❏ 18:4–8

❏ 18:9, 10 ❏ 18:11–13

3 What do the woman and Babylon represent? What about our society fits the description of Babylon?

_____

_____

_____

_____

4 What sin underlies all of the evil acts described here? How does the kingdom of this world differ from the Kingdom of God?

_____

_____

_____

_____

5 What is it about the woman that is so attractive? When we think of evil, something ugly or distasteful often comes to mind. How can evil appear to be attractive in your life?

_____

_____

_____

_____

In the Bible, Babylon symbolizes the evil system of this world. This section describes the wickedness of Babylon, especially its materialism, and its ultimate demise. First-century readers immediately would have thought of Rome. The Roman Empire had grown rich through greed and by exploiting sinful pleasures. Many governments and lives are built on greed and the lust for power. As powerful and impressive as it all is, however, the evil system of this world will one day come to an end. Rome fell, and so will every city, institution, and individual that sets itself against God. Are you living for the Kingdom of God or for the kingdom of this world?

REALIZE
the principle

6 Beauty and pleasure often cover the horrendous reality of evil. What evil in your society has been made appealing with an attractive cover?

_____

_____

_____

_____

7 Consider how the various parties react to the fall of Babylon. Why do they mourn? What do they miss most about Babylon?

_____

_____

_____

_____

RESPOND
to the message

8 What has been God's attitude toward Babylon, and how does that explain his actions?

_____

_____

_____

9 If you had been one of the people spoken of in 18:4, what would have been your reaction? ("I'm so surprised!" "Wait a minute, let me pack." "Well, it's about time." "Oh, those poor people—if they'd only listened!")

_____

_____

_____

_____

10 As a citizen of the Kingdom of God, where have you felt pressured to adopt the lifestyle of the kingdom of Babylon?

_____

_____

_____

_____

11 How does this picture of Babylon give you a new perspective of the world and its values?

_____

_____

_____

_____

RESOLVE
to take action

12 How much of your life are you investing in succeeding in this world, in making it in the world's system? What are your current goals in life? What changes should you make to invest in the Kingdom of God instead?

_____

_____

_____

_____

A Why would people in John's day need this description of Babylon to see the decay in the Roman Empire? What sort of perspective do you need to see the way sin rules your world?

MORE
for studying
other themes
in this section

B Read some of the other episodes in the Bible where God destroyed evil cities. Tyre (Ezekiel 26—28); Babylon (Isaiah 13—14; 21; Jeremiah 50—51); Sodom and Gomorrah (Genesis 19); Chorazin and Bethsaida (Matthew 11:21). What was it about these cities that deserved God's wrath? How does each one serve as a mirror for what God will do to the whole world? What sort of message does each destruction deliver?

C Compare this message of judgment with the message to and reaction of the people of Nineveh in the book of Jonah.

D What does the phrase "she was drunk . . . with the blood of God's holy people" mean? How does this continue today?

REFLECT
on your life

1 If someone asked you why God allows evil in the world, how would you answer?

_____

_____

_____

_____

_____

2 What evil in the world sometimes makes you wonder if God is really in control of everything?

_____

_____

_____

_____

3 How has evil impacted your life in a way that made you question the power and authority of God?

_____

_____

_____

_____

_____

Read Revelation 19:1—20:15 and the following notes:

❐ 19:1ff ❐ 19:1–8 ❐ 19:10 ❐ 19:11–21 ❐ 20:2–4 ❐ 20:3 ❐ 20:5, 6

❐ 20:6 ❐ 20:9 ❐ 20:10 ❐ 20:14

READ
the passage

4 Why did John want to worship the angel (19:10)? What does the angel's response tell us about a believer's identity?

_____

_____

_____

5 Who is the rider on the white horse? What is the significance of the sharp sword?

_____

_____

6 What is the ultimate end of Satan and all who follow him?

_____

_____

7 What is the difference between the first death and the second death?

_____

_____

8 What does the future hold for all of those who follow Christ?

_____

_____

_____

In this section, the great multitude shouts praises for the fall of Babylon; Christ defeats all of his foes; Satan is imprisoned for the thousand years and then destroyed; and the dead are judged. Thus evil is eliminated and eradicated from the heavens and the earth. God permits evil now, but he will not always allow evil to coexist with good. Ultimately, Satan and all that is evil will be destroyed. We should remember this and take courage when we feel over-whelmed by the evil in the world. Knowing that you are on the winning side, you can have hope in the midst of hopeless times and situations.

REALIZE
the principle

9 Jesus will establish a whole new order of life without the evil influences and hindrances of Satan. How will that be different than life as you know it today?

_____

_____

_____

_____

_____

RESPOND
to the message

10 What evil influences are you going to be most relieved to see removed from the earth?

_____

_____

_____

_____

11 What is there in your life that would cause you to say, "Wait, I'm not yet ready for this to be over"? What makes you apprehensive about Christ's return?

_____

_____

_____

12 Why does the concept of a final judgment make some people so uncomfortable? How do you feel when you read about this judgment?

_____

_____

_____

_____

_____

13 What about your battle against sin and evil is the most discouraging? In what areas have you given up the struggle?

_____

_____

_____

_____

14 Select one area where you need to step up your fight against evil in your life or against satanic influence around you. How hard are you fighting that battle right now? Why have you decreased your efforts lately? What do you want to do differently, keeping the outcome of the final battle in mind?

RESOLVE
to take action

_____

_____

_____

_____

_____

A What is there about the rider (19:11) that reveals his identity? How would you respond if you were to see Christ like that right now?

MORE
for studying
other themes
in this section

B Evaluate the weapons carried by Christ as the rider. Where are they named elsewhere in Scripture? How are they available to us today? How does Jesus use these weapons in your life today?

C Read through Ephesians 5:25–27 and then go back to the comparison of the evil woman of Revelation 17 and the bride of Revelation 19. How is your church like the bride? How could you help make the bride more beautiful?

D Review the battles in 16:12–16; 17:14–16; and 20:7–10. How are they similar? How are they different? What does the final battle tell us about our daily battles?

E What would a Christian in John's day learn by comparing the character of the woman in chapter 17 with the bride of Christ (19:6–9)? How might that affect the way Christians throughout history view themselves?

F What is the purpose behind the battles in 19:19–21 and 20:9? How does the study note on 20:3 help you understand God's actions here? How does God confirm our relationship with him?

G What are the differences between the postmillennial, premillennial, and amillennial interpretations of the thousand-year reign of Christ in 20:1–6?

LESSON 12
TURN YOUR HEART TOWARD HEAVEN
REVELATION 21:1—22:6

REFLECT
on your life

1 When you were a child, what did you think heaven would be like?

_____

_____

_____

_____

_____

2 List the popular misconceptions of heaven as portrayed by television, movies, and so forth (for example, harps, wings, clouds).

_____

_____

_____

_____

READ
the passage

Read Revelation 21:1—22:6, "The Beginning and the End" and "What We Know about Eternity" charts, and the following notes:

❒ 21:1　❒ 21:2, 3　❒ 21:3, 4　❒ 21:5　❒ 21:7, 8　❒ 21:10ff　❒ 21:12–14

❒ 21:18–21　❒ 21:22–24　❒ 22:2

3 How do each of the items in the chart "The Beginning and the End" give believers hope for the future?

_____

_____

_____

_____

4 Why is a temple not needed in the new city? What does this say about the relationship we will have with God?

_____

_____

_____

_____

5 What do you see as the most interesting and attractive feature in the description of the new Jerusalem? What makes you want to live there?

_____

_____

_____

_____

This section tells us of the new heaven and the new earth. This vision of eternity can be reassuring. Heaven is not merely an extension of life right now; it is a new creation, a fresh start. It's not a dream world filled with spirit-beings, but a vivid, striking, light-filled city. Some people are not eager to go to heaven. Perhaps they fear the unknown, or they have misconceptions from childhood and the media, or they are having fun on earth. This accurate description of heaven may change your perspective. Those who don't find the prospect of heaven exciting just may not be very interested in being close to God for such a long time.

REALIZE
the principle

6 Christians in John's day were experiencing great pain and persecution. How are God's people experiencing such pain today? Where in the world are believers facing heavy persecution?

_____

_____

_____

_____

_____

7 What does this description of the new Jerusalem suggest about what life will be like in eternity?

_____

_____

_____

_____

8 How does reading the ending help us live here and now?

_____

_____

_____

_____

9 What is so reassuring to believers about a new heaven and a new earth?

_____

_____

_____

_____

RESPOND
to the message

10 How does this picture of heaven compare to the misconceptions you listed at the beginning of this lesson?

_____

_____

_____

_____

11 Of all the facts you have discovered about eternity, what do you look forward to the most?

_____

_____

_____

_____

12 What misconceptions about heaven do you need to change in your mind? What bad attitudes do you need to examine more closely?

_____

_____

_____

_____

13 As we experience the troubles and trials of each day, it's difficult to keep eternity in mind. What can you do this week to keep your heart turned toward heaven?

RESOLVE
to take action

_____

_____

_____

_____

_____

A Compare the features of the new Jerusalem to other areas of Scripture listed in the study notes (Genesis 1—3; Ezekiel 47:1-2; Joel 3:18; Zechariah 14:8). How do the features of the city explain what we will experience in heaven?

MORE
for studying
other themes
in this section

B Compare this vision of the new Jerusalem with the visions from Ezekiel 40—48 and Isaiah 60—66. What are the similarities and significant differences? What new information do we receive through John?

C Why is there no temple in the new Jerusalem? What does this say about the type of worship Jesus describes in John 4 as worshiping in spirit and in truth?

D Describe what worship will be like in heaven. How can we anticipate that in the worship we experience here on earth?

E We are promised that God will wipe away all tears and that there will be no more death, sorrow, crying, or pain (21:4). What events have caused you great sorrow during the past year? How will heaven turn your sorrow into joy?

F How would you explain heaven to a non-Christian? to a blind person?

LESSON 13
I AM COMING SOON
REVELATION 22:7–21

REFLECT
on your life

1 What is something that you are waiting for that you wish would arrive or happen more quickly?

_____

_____

_____

_____

2 What has been one of the most difficult things in your life to wait for?

_____

_____

_____

_____

READ
the passage

Read Revelation 22:7–21 and the following notes:

❏ 22:8, 9　❏ 22:10, 11　❏ 22:12–14　❏ 22:17　❏ 22:18, 19　❏ 22:20　❏ 22:21

3 How many times in this section did Jesus say that he was coming soon?

_____

_____

_____

4 How could his return have been soon in A.D. 95 and also today?

_____

_____

_____

REALIZE
the principle

When a computer takes more than a few seconds to perform a task, we say it is slow. When it prints the page in only a few seconds, we say it is fast. When a car drives 90 miles per hour, we say it is going fast. When a plane flies 90 miles per hour, we say it is going slow. Speed is relative—a matter of perspective and expectations. Jesus is not being slow in his return, and he will come soon. We may wonder why we have had to wait almost 2000 years for Christ to return. But when your life is over, and you are in heaven, you just might say to yourself, "That sure went fast."

5 What kinds of events in your life make Jesus' return seem slow in coming?

_____

_____

_____

_____

6 God's people are urged to wash their robes (22:14). What robes are to be washed? How are they washed? What are the benefits to washing their robes? What would washing mean to Christians in John's day?

_____

_____

_____

_____

RESPOND
to the message

7 When will it be too late for people to change? Why are we able to change now? What reasons do people give to avoid changing their attitudes and behavior?

_____

_____

_____

_____

8 How prepared do you feel for Christ's coming? What could you do to be more prepared?

_____

_____

_____

_____

9 When life is going well and holds much promise for us, we are not eager for Christ to return just yet. But when we are suffering intensely, we want him to come right away. How eager are you for Christ to return?

_____

_____

_____

RESOLVE
to take action

10 When unhealthy ambitions or desires get in the way of our relationship with Christ, we often do not want him to return soon. What in your heart blocks your desire to be with God? What priorities do you need to adjust?

_____

_____

_____

_____

MORE
for studying
other themes
in this section

A Why are those who keep the words of the prophecy in this book blessed?

B Why was it wrong for John to worship the angel? What kinds of things are Christians tempted to worship today?

C The Trinity is seen throughout the book of Revelation. How are Father, Son, and Holy Spirit described in Revelation 1:4, 5? How are they described in Revelation 22:6, 9, 16, 17? What is the role of each Person?

D What does it mean to not seal up the words of this book (22:10)? How does this differ from the vision that Daniel received?

E How can people add to or take away from the words of the Bible?

F There are seven blessings pronounced in Revelation, two of which are in chapter 22 (1:3; 14:13; 16:15; 19:9; 20:6; 22:7, 14). What must a believer do to receive these blessings?

G What does it mean to be thirsty for the water of life? How does a person increase this thirst?

H Go through the names of Jesus in Revelation 22:12–17. How does the picture of the future that you have seen in Revelation help you understand what these names mean? What is the significance of these names for your life right now?

I Having read through the book of Revelation, go through the following list and write down the new discoveries you have made and the difference each discovery has made in your attitude and life.

	Discovery	*Difference*
Jesus	_____	_____
	_____	_____
Satan	_____	_____
	_____	_____
Heaven	_____	_____
	_____	_____
Hell	_____	_____
	_____	_____
Judgment	_____	_____
	_____	_____
Persecution	_____	_____
	_____	_____
Suffering	_____	_____
	_____	_____
Evil	_____	_____
	_____	_____
Holiness	_____	_____
	_____	_____
Worship	_____	_____